WORDS *of* HOPE *for* ALL TIMES

Words of Hope
For you
Isaiah 41:10
W.E. Berg

WORDS *of* HOPE *for* ALL TIMES

From Life and The Book of Life

WILLIAM E. BERG

BRONZE BOW  PUBLISHING

WORDS *of* HOPE *for* ALL TIMES

Published by Bronze Bow Publishing LLC.
Minneapolis, Minnesota

Printed by Sentinel Printing, St. Cloud, Minnesota
ISBN 0-9715299-6-5

TABLE OF CONTENTS

DEDICATION

To my great grandchildren,
Maya Carlson and Emery Carlson

Nurtured by words of hope by parents and grandparents, they face not an easy future, but a destiny to bless and serve many with love. They are forever safe, not in my arms but in the arms of Jesus.

PREFACE

✝

DURING THE YEARS OF 1965 TO 1980 I SERVED AS PASTOR OF
the Augustana Lutheran Church in Minneapolis, Minnesota. For
the first five years of this ministry, the church sponsored a monthly
publication entitled, "The Augustana Messenger". During the years
from 1970 to 1980, we also sponsored a weekly publication, "The
Good News". During this decade, I wrote some 400 weekly messages. In a review of many of them I discovered that they reflected
not only the needs and trends of that day but also the challenges of
my day. With the help of an outstanding editorial committee, whose
members were not reluctant to provide unbiased appraisal, the messages were reviewed. The committee selected 40 of the messages for
publication in this book.

In that decade we were trying to recover from "the tumultuous
60's" highlighted (or frequently lowlighted!) by the philosophy of
"doing your own thing", and being free to be the person you are
without regard for trying to be the person you ought to be for the
best interest of all persons.

For example, I recall an encounter with some young people who
came to our parking lot during our summer Crossroad outreach
ministry. They said words to this effect: "The world would be better
off without this church and all of these do-good church people". My
answer in effect was this: "Every day in this place we are giving food
for the body and spiritual nurture for the spirit, sponsoring interest
and achievement groups such as cooking, auto mechanics and many
others, hosting twice weekly drama and entertainment on the
Crossroad stage, counseling families in need, especially mothers, taking children and youth from the inner city to summer camps". They
were totally unimpressed by this recital. When I invited them to join
us and help in these ministries, they walked away.

But they surely taught me something that day. I thought about
the need of the church to minister to precisely these young people

who are turned off by the church and who rightfully expose some of our weaknesses and neglects. I should have invited them to one of our worship services where we preach the good news of regeneration and salvation for all sinners, including those young people and myself, and also the good news that we are called by our Lord to social action and ministry for those in need.

And now I give a special tribute to members of the editorial committee. They are Katherine Krause, Don and Karin Goodell, Carol Smith, Anne Carlson, Karen Balmer, Jon Carlson, Jeff Carlson, Trey and Jackie Bailey and Katie Schoeppner. All of them have been indispensable partners but especially Katie Schoeppner, who has spent hours beyond counting using her professional skills typing and re-typing this manusscript.

It gives me deep joy to include four of Marta Berg's poems in this book. She shares the transforming power of divine hope in a few eloquent lines, a gift of the Spirit indeed. It takes me many more words, even pages, to express the same thoughts.

For the last twelve years God has given me the great gift of partnership with Duff Smith and Koechel Peterson & Associates who have designed the covers of all of my books. If readers will study these covers that are reproduced in this book, they will sense that the designers must have indeed been led by the Holy Spirit to design so that readers get the message of the Lord clearly by the message of the covers. Partnership with them in design and layout has been one of the big blessings of my writing career.

I must admit that in this two-year process doubts have often come to burden my spirit. I thought, "Would readers by interested in these messages?" Each one is only a page and one half in length. Each one stands on its own without any attempt to classify them under general themes. I remember sharing some of these doubts and burdens with my family. They kept encouraging me, saying by all means they should be published. I recall my granddaughter Katie, who is now doing her graduate studies in social work at the University of Minnesota, preaching "a powerful sermon" to me telling why she believed this book should be written.

Here I will add a note to the readers: Biblical references alone are often given throughout the text. Hopefully this will encourage many readers to use this book as a study guide for getting deeper into scripture.

The most important incentive in continuing this ministry, especially at the age of 97, is that the more I prayed daily about this book the more peace I received from the Lord.

The "I will" promises from my Lord kept me going:

"I will instruct you and teach you the way that you should go;
I will counsel you with my eye upon you."
PSALM 32:8

"Fear not, for I am with you;
be not dismayed, for I am your God.
I will strengthen you, I will help you,
I will uphold you with my victorious right hand."
ISAIAH 41:10

Hopefully the title of this book will appeal to readers. Loss of hope and optimism is one of the tragic realities of our day. We are in the midst of an unwinnable war in Iraq. Economic recession seems to be eminent. Nations are rising against nations in civil wars, killing countless persons. Terrorists are lurking everywhere seeking to destroy.

I should also add that I am writing this Preface in the midst of an unprecedented political campaign for the office of the President of the United States. Each day we hear torrents of words from the candidates telling of their hopes and plans for our country and also parading their talents. I am grateful that I live in a democracy where we have freedom of speech and so many other freedoms. But I sometimes wonder what our Lord thinks about all these words that are spoken. Some of them do reflect ideas that would be for the good of the country. But why does He not hear and why do we not hear challenges and reminders of our historic heritage—"One Nation Under God"?

In one of the poems from her book, *From Grey to Gold,* my life-partner, Marta, tells of a lady who got on a city bus, bypassing the fare box. The driver reminded her of her neglect. She said, "But driver, I'm only going six blocks." This was his response: "Anyone who rides has got to pay." Marta follows through with these thoughts:

"You have to study and think in order to grow as a person. You have to move out of the easy chair to know the joy of widening horizons and a fuller life. You have to know the pain of caring to have the joy of helping others. You have to practice the presence of God in order to know His will and His way. You have to give love before you can know friendship in depth."

In other words caring is a costly business and caring words do not come cheap.

Marta concludes with these words: "The scriptural basis for this truth is graphically told in the words 'Looking to Jesus... who for the JOY that was set before Him endured the cross, despising the shame.'" Hebrews 12:2.

INTRODUCTION

MANY READERS WILL PROBABLY THINK THAT THE introduction to my new book begins in a strange way. In October of 2007 I shared the following message at the marriage service of my grandson, Steven Conrad, and his bride, Emily Behr:

> Steve and Emily, I have high hopes for you. Here are some of them:
>
> I hope for you a journey of growth in knowledge of who you are and why you are unbreakably joined together for life at this holy altar.
>
> I hope that divine grace will uphold you as together you experience inevitable problems and burdens in a dangerous and fallen world.
>
> I hope that you will deeply sense the continuing and surrounding love and prayers of your family and friends.
>
> I hope that your arms will often enfold each other in a fond embrace, yes, and that someday your arms will enfold beautiful babies, God's special gift to you.

But now I must remind you that my words of hope cannot give you what they express to you. You need divine words. A story may help us at this point.

It's the story of a bride and groom at the altar. During the service, the bride was indeed beautiful, calm and poised, but the bridegroom was very nervous. He fidgeted and moved his hands in and out of his pockets. The best man whispered, "John, what happened? Did you lose the ring?" John replied, "Worse than that, I've lost my enthusiasm!"

The word "enthusiasm" comes from the Greek "en" and "theos", "in God". You need "in God" and "in Jesus" words. For example, words found in Jeremiah 29:11:

"For I know the plans I have for you, says the Lord,
plans for welfare and not for evil,
to give you a future and a hope."

Let us pray. We thank you, our blessed Lord, that as Steve and Emily walk down this aisle into their future life together, we see Jesus, their Lord and Saviour, walking with them. As they walk together, we thank you for your words of hope that you are giving to them. We thank you for their beautiful foot washing service that reveals to us their servant role of self-giving service for persons in need in their community, in the Congo and across the world. Thank you, Lord, for giving divine words of hope to all of us, sustaining us in our life journey until you come to take us Home.

Hopefully this message contains themes related to the title of this book, *Words of Hope for All Times.*

Times of joy and times of sorrow. Times of burdens and blessings. Times of suffering and pain and times of health and vigor.

If we have a realistic perspective of our fallen world, readers will understand why the word "All" is so important in this book.

Words of hope for the dying. Words from Jesus our Saviour and Lord:

"Jesus said to her, I am the resurrection and the life;
he who believes in me though he die, yet shall he live,
and whoever lives and believes in me shall never die..."
JOHN 11:25,26

Words of hope for persons severely impaired in body and spirit:

"...My grace is sufficient for you
for my power is made perfect in weakness..."
II CORINTHIANS 12:9

Words of hope about Jesus who suffered terrifying and excruciating pain and agony in Gethsemane and on the cross to give us this reassuring word:

"Therefore, since we are justified by faith, we have peace with God through our Lord Jesus Christ. Through him we have obtained access to this grace in which we stand, and we rejoice in our hope of sharing the glory of God. More than that, we rejoice in our sufferings, knowing that suffering produces endurance, and endurance produces character, and character produces hope."
ROMANS 5:1-5

More words of hope from our Lord:

"And there will be signs in sun and moon and stars, and upon the earth distress of nations in perplexity at the roaring of the sea and the waves, men fainting with fear and with foreboding of what is coming on the world; for the powers of the heavens will be shaken. And then they will see the Son of man coming in a cloud with power and great glory. Now when these things begin to take place, look up and raise your heads, because your redemption is drawing near."
LUKE 21:25-28

It was 2,000 years ago that Jesus predicted the tragedies that would happen even in our present day. But in the midst of Jesus' message about the tragedies that will happen, we have His reassuring words of hope, "Look up, your redemption is drawing near."

Words of hope for all times. Yes, and for the crisis times in the year 2007 during which this book is written. Here is a partial list of present day crises:

- War in Iraq and the Middle East
- The AIDS epidemic
- Nuclear proliferation
- Global warming
- Internet exploitation of children
- Wanton consumerism
- Human rights crises

- Destruction of the environment by human greed
- Land mines littering the landscape of many nations
- Widespread world hunger and malnutrition crises
- The crisis of political expediency in which persons are expendable
- The illusion that military might is the way to peace
- Terrorism stalking at the doors of many nations

It is important for the Church of Jesus Christ to recall the meaning of the word crisis. It has a double connotation; danger and opportunity. Indeed there are dangers in the Church today; among them efforts to change the divine design for marriage and ignoring the sanctity of life. Also, we face the danger of accepting the gospel of cheap grace in the place of costly discipleship. In the church we also face a "Crisis of Christology" in which Jesus as the fulfillment of all Truth and as Final Authority is rejected.

In the midst of these crises we turn to divine words of hope. The divine word of hope is a word of faith:

"May the God of hope fill you with all joy and peace in believing, so that by the power of the Holy Spirit you may abound in hope."
ROMANS 15:13 RSV

"If my people who are called by my name humble themselves, and pray and seek my face, and turn from their wicked ways, then I will hear from heaven, and will forgive their sin and heal their land."
II CHRONICLES 7:14

For those who are going down into hopelessness and despair there is a great word of hope in I Peter 5:6,7:

"Humble yourselves, therefore, under the mighty hand of God, that in due time he may exalt you. Cast all your anxieties on him, for he cares about you."

When we go down under the mighty hand of God, and even when His hand seems to be pressing us down, we need to remember that we go down under His hand only to be lifted higher. It is the same hand that was nailed to a cruel cross of torture and shame to rescue us and to give us words of hope.

Oftentimes in this fallen world we have to wait for the fulfillment of our hopes. We read in Psalm 39:7:

"And now, Lord, for what do I wait? My hope is in thee."

There is a powerful word of hope for those who are waiting for the fulfillment of their hopes. It is found in Isaiah 40:31:

"But they who wait for the Lord shall renew their strength,
they shall mount up with wings like eagles,
they shall run and not be weary, they shall walk and not faint."

In other words they shall keep on waiting until they experience the fulfillment of their hopes according to the Word of God.

Is there hope in the midst of earthquakes and other calamities of nature that kill millions of persons? We need to remember an earthquake that happened 2,000 years ago on a hillside outside the walls of Jerusalem. Jesus Christ, Son of God, Creator of the Universe, was hanging on the cross, crucified for the sins of the human race. When Jesus had been on His cross for several hours, an earthquake shook the world. But in this earthquake no lives were lost except the life of the Son of God. In this earthquake came the promise of new life and hope for all who believe. Here we have a calming word of hope in the midst of calamity.

It is true that our human words, words of sympathy and empathy, words of compassion (suffering with) can be used to bring hope to many persons in need, especially when these words are accompanied by self-giving service, love with embracing arms.

However, our human words can never lift anyone into their highest hopes and dreams, never into sustaining, upholding grace in every circumstance. Divine words, holy words and the promises of the Bible alone can bring undying hope for time and eternity.

Above all, we need the word of the cross of Jesus to give us hope that never fails.

It is good for us to affirm the words of the hymn "My Hope is Built on Nothing Less":

> My hope is built on nothing less
>   Than Jesus' blood and righteousness:
> No merit of my own I claim,
>   But wholly lean on Jesus' name.
>
> When darkness veils His lovely face,
>   I rest on His unchanging grace;
> In every high and stormy gale,
>   my anchor holds within the veil.
>
> When I shall launch to worlds unseen,
>   O may I then be found in Him!
> Dressed in His righteousness alone,
>   Faultless to stand before the throne.
>
> Chorus: On Christ, the solid Rock I stand,
>   All other ground is sinking sand.

Coming back to my words of hope shared with Steve and Emily at the beginning of this introduction, I should have added a word of warning for them. In this fallen, sin-cursed world theirs will be a very costly journey.

I am reminded of the bridegroom who asked the officiating pastor at the end of their marriage ceremony, "How much do I owe you?" The pastor replied, "Whatever you think it's worth." The bridegroom handed the pastor a one dollar bill and the pastor gave him fifty cents in change!

Both Steve and Emily are called by their Lord and Savior to be His disciples. And discipleship is very costly in our world.

But I know they are willing to pay the price because they believe in the word of hope given to them from the Holy Book in II Corinthians 12:9:

> *"My grace is sufficient for you,*
> *for my power is made perfect in weakness."*

I close this introduction with four poems written by my life partner Marta. She left us for her heavenly home in 1996, but not before blessing family and countless friends with her words of faith and hope and love. Her books of narrative verse, *Seen and Unseen* and *From Grey to Gold*, give us four poems that I believe will bless and challenge all readers. I may be accused of prejudice but I say without apology that these are the best books of narrative verse I have ever read.

COSTLY WORDS
MARTA'S POEM ENTITLED "THEFT"

There are those who steal silver and gold,
and there are those who steal
the most precious commodity of all —
the life of another.
Not with gun,
nor with axe,
but with words
and with scorn.
They diminish life bit by bit,
robbing another
of tranquility
and joy
and dignity,
by complaining,
demeaning,
scolding,
mocking,
nagging.
Their name, too, is "Thief."

Jesus said:

"I tell you, on the day of judgment men will render account
for every careless word they utter; for by your words
you will be justified, and by your words you will be condemned."
MATTHEW 12:36,37

A HUMBLING, COMFORTING AND UNMERITED WORD
MARTA'S POEM ENTITLED "A WORD"

Someone said it,
"God is like Mount Everest,
and I'm a Tonka toy car
trying to get to the top."
Not so!
Jesus gave us a word
that puts us in
awesome nearness
to the Creator of the universe,
the Maker of all time and space,
the One whose majesty fills all of
sky and sea and land.
It is a humbling word,
a comforting word,
an unmerited word.
The word is,
"Father."
God...my Father!

"Thou art my father, my God,
and the rock of my salvation."
PSALM 89:26

A REASSURING WORD
MARTA'S POEM ENTITLED "SURELY"

Surely goodness and mercy
shall follow me...
There was that word again—surely.
How can anyone say surely in a day of
tumultuous change?
Or had the Psalmist noted
that there is an absolute certainty
in the universe,
that God's law is unfailingly constant?
On the strength of its constancy,
persons can leave Earth and function in space.
The nurtured bud always opens into bloom.
Ice always forms at the freezing point.
Gravity never takes a vacation.
And so it is with God's moral law...
Repentance gives birth to joy.
Peace is a partner of trust.
Love opens doors closed by hate.
God's certainties are written into
the very heartbeat of life itself.
Yes, SURELY.

"Surely he has borne our griefs and carried or sorrows;
yet we esteemed him stricken, smitten by God, and afflicted."
ISAIAH 53:4

A WORD WITH POWER
TO CHANGE THE WORLD
MARTA'S POEM ENTITLED "A MAID AND A CARPENTER"

"Do you know what I want to be when I grow up?"
It was a four-year-old's question.
"No. What?"
"A maid, cause then I can make everything
In the world
Sparkly clean."
Her brothers quickly disillusioned her.
They gave a recital of the hard realities
Of low pay and onerous work.
Because of two little boys
The world lost its chance to become "sparkly clean."
But a man was sent to earth
With a plan and with power,
Awesome power
To sweep clean every human heart,
Priest and publican alike.
That one who changed the world was a carpenter.
Even now He has the power to change the world
Or to change one life.
You and I can know this power.
LOVE is its name.

> *"Create in me a clean heart, O God,*
> *and put a new and right spirit within me.*
> *Cast me not away from thy presence,*
> *and take not thy Holy Spirit from me."*
> PSALM 50:10,11

WORDS *of* HOPE *for* ALL TIMES

A LESSON FROM JOHNNY AND SOME SQUEAKY SHOES

✝

ONE SUMMER, MY WIFE MARTA AND I DROVE TO DENVER to visit our daughter, her husband and their three-year-old son, Jon. We wondered if he would recognize us from a visit in our home a year before. Sad to say, he gave no sign of recognition. He kept on munching cookies until Marta walked across the room with her comfortable but very squeaky sandals. Jon listened and said, "Mormor" (grandma in Swedish). He recognized her by the squeak heard during a Minneapolis visit.

Recognized by a squeak! Well, that's better than not being recognized at all. But soon Jon and Marta and I were getting acquainted again.

Perhaps this question is in order. What is the characteristic by which you are known or recognized? Is it a smile? A happy greeting? Is it a frown or a complaining word? Are people made glad wherever you go or *whenever* you go?

I will always remember Jimmy Breed, a man afflicted with epilepsy and deformity at Bethphage Mission, a Christian home for persons with physical, mental and emotional problems. In the midst of his crippled and twisted body and his slurred speech, I catch the key-note of Jimmy's life. Each time I come, Jimmy, with great difficulty, gets these words out, "**Pastor Berg, Keep Looking Up!**" That's how I know and recognize him best—by the picture of a bent-over, afflicted man looking up.

God offers to each child of His a magnificent mark of distinction. He offers His best gift—the Holy Spirit—Jesus' Love and Power within! He offers to let the beauty of Jesus shine through you and out from your life.

When Marta comes I do not say, "Here comes Squeaky." I say, "Here comes a beautiful person." I know her by her love. May all people know we are Christians by our love!

I hope people will recognize me as belonging to God, not by clerical collar, but because Jesus lives within me.

AFFIRMATION
Interesting characteristics are good, but I prefer
the character that only God can create.

MORE WORDS OF HOPE
"I have been crucified with Christ; it is no longer
I who live, but Christ who lives in me; and the life
I now live in the flesh I live by faith in the Son of God,
who loved me and gave himself for me."
GALATIANS 2:20

ARE WE LOSING SOMETHING?

✝

THERE IS A TRAGIC LOSS THAT IS HURTING THE CHURCH today and limiting our service to God. It is the loss of a **Sense of Wonder**—the loss of a sense of awe and amazement in the presence of true greatness—in the presence of God. Think of objects of awe and wonder. We look at a baby with a sense of wonder. (It easily turns into a nightmare of contradiction as a baby left to die of exposure is called a crime, and a baby destroyed in its mother's womb is called freedom of choice!) There's the wonder of a sunset, a rainbow, the ocean and many other wonders. But now we speak not of wonders, but of the **Wonder of Wonders**.

Here is the **Wonder of Wonders—the Wonder of Jesus becoming one of us**. He was alone in the wilderness. He was hungry. He was weak in body. He became a man of sorrows and acquainted with grief. He experienced firsthand the demonic deceptions of the devil. He knows that we are no match for this enemy. How does He know? He became one of us. "Surely, He has borne our griefs and carried our sorrows." Isaiah 53:4.

Some birds on a bitterly cold and stormy night were flying against the picture window of a home. The man inside turned off the light. Still they came and he thought, "I must do something. They will kill themselves." He went to the barn, turned on the lights there and left the door wide open. They still flew against that picture window. They were dropping dead one by one. The man said, "There is only one way to save them. If I could become a bird and speak their language and teach them, I could save them."

Wonder of Wonders! Jesus became one of us. He even became sin for us that we might become the righteousness of God through Him. In your hurting and physical pain, under your heavy load of grief, in the midst of your temptations, fears and frustrations, remember Jesus has become one with you. He understands. He has been through it all.

AFFIRMATION
I am saved, a saved sinner, but also lost,
lost in wonder, love and praise.

MORE WORDS OF HOPE
"And the Word became flesh and dwelt among us,
full of grace and truth; we have beheld his glory,
glory as of the only Son from the Father."
JOHN 1:14

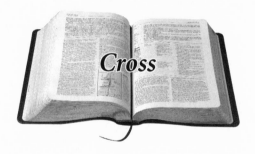

ARE YOU A POSSIBILITY THINKER?

ONCE I HEARD A PASTOR TELL THE STORY OF AN INCENTIVE session for salesmen. It seems that several hundred salesmen were giving all kinds of excuses as to why they could not meet the goals set for them. They all said, "It's impossible." Their supervisor, after listening the entire afternoon to their pleas for attainable goals, abruptly dismissed them with the words, "That's all for today. Come back tomorrow at noon."

He quickly contacted the heads of several companies and persuaded them to demolish the headquarters building, fill the hole and level the ground, cut the grass on several acres of farmland, roll up hundreds of yards of sod, bring in 200 potted geranium plans and turn the land on which the building had stood into a beautiful lawn and garden. All this was accomplished in about 15 hours of time with tractors, searchlights and special equipment.

When the salesmen came the next day at noon they were astonished, bewildered and confused at what they saw. Their supervisor appeared and said, "Ladies and Gentlemen, what you see here will tell you that nothing is impossible—nothing!" The meeting adjourned with that speech. Within a short time every salesman had exceeded the impossible quota!

We should marvel at the "impossible" achievements of mortal man. But I am quite unmoved by possibility thinking that is rooted only in human cleverness and ingenuity. For what shall it profit if we land on the moon while destroying ourselves on this planet earth by our infected attitudes and polluted souls?

When Jesus Christ died for our sins, and rose to make new persons of us **on the inside**, He accomplished the most impossible of all miracles. Someone has said, "The Church is made up of believers who have had God do the impossible in their lives—forgive sin, cleanse, restore, heal, make all things new." Remember, with God all things are possible. All things!

AFFIRMATION
God can turn my problems into possibilities.
I thank him for the great exchange.

MORE WORDS OF HOPE
"But Jesus looked at them and said to them,
'With men this is impossible,
but with God all things are possible.'"
MATTHEW 19:26

Mercy

BLESSING
IN BOSTON

✝

IN 1971 IT WAS MY PRIVILEGE TO SPEND SEVERAL HOURS with Dr. E. Stanley Jones, world missionary and evangelist who preached 60,000 sermons on all seven continents. He was in the Massachusetts Rehabilitation Center in Boston, seeking health and restoration following a stroke.

For some 35 years I have been inspired by his books, and his messages heard in person have lifted and challenged me. But on that day many years ago, I heard his greatest message, his pulpit a hospital bed, his body stricken, his speech faltering, with every word coming with effort. Here are excerpts from his eloquent sermon: "Nothing has changed. I'm the same person...I belong to the unshakable Kingdom and to the unchanging Person...He may heal; He may not, but I believe in the divine **yes**...I see an open door. Perhaps it's to write a book from here...This is not the end, but the beginning...Jesus is Lord!"

Then we put our hands upon him and sang, "O For a Thousand Tongues to Sing My Dear Redeemer's Name". Dr. Jones sang with us. A hallowed moment indeed!

In a letter I told Dr. Jones of the little boy who was asked, "Sonny, who made you?" The little fellow replied indignantly, "Mister, I ain't done yet!" There is more to be done for His glory! The boiler may be in for repairs but the fire of the Spirit burns brightly.

We had a party in Dr. Jones' hospital room on his 88th birthday. He said, "It's fun to be 88 and it's getting funnier all the time!" Life in Jesus Christ gives more fun, more satisfaction, more celebration, more endurance, more hope, more power to make life count for others, and more excitement about what's ahead.

At that time I shared with Dr. Jones the feeling that this present chapter in his life may well be climaxed by his presence and witness for Christ at the World Ashram Congress in Jerusalem and Galilee, June 25-29, 1972. His doctors had said that he would never walk or travel again. But he was there in a wheelchair with two nurses in attendance. In giving the keynote address to 325 delegates to the International Christian Ashram in Jerusalem, his powerful one hour message, even given with slurred speech, was memorable. I introduced him with the story of a little boy who came to him following a sermon. He asked if he could shake hands with Dr. Jones, who offered his hand. The boy kept shaking his hand and then said, "Dr. Jones, shaking hands with you is the second greatest honor of my life." When asked about his greatest honor, he replied, "Shaking hands with Joe Louis." (Heavy weight champion boxer of the world!) I recall saying that night, "Dr. Jones, knowing you as my teacher and mentor has been one of the greatest honors of my life."

AFFIRMATION
My greatest honor: To be chosen to worship the living
God, and chosen for fruitful service in His kingdom.

MORE WORDS OF HOPE
"You did not choose me, but I chose you and
appointed you that you should go and bear fruit
and that your fruit should abide; so that whatever you
ask the Father in my name, he may give it to you."
JOHN 15:16

Grace

COME AND SEE
FOR YOURSELF

LET ME SHARE WITH YOU THE EXCITEMENT AND enthusiasm—yes, and the incredible optimism I feel about the distinctive approach of the Gospel of Jesus Christ to hearts and minds. It is this: "**Come and See**". In St. John's gospel, chapter one, verses 39 and 46, we read of Philip meeting the Messiah, and saying to Nathanael, who doubted that anything good could come out of Nazareth, "**Come and See!**" An honest and authentic man of science, no matter what he may think, is bound to put evidence to the test—to **Come and See**.

The late Dr. E. Stanley Jones tells of the man who turns his back on the sunset. Listening to a friend describing its magnificent, breathtaking beauty, he refuses to turn and look. He just says, "I don't believe it." A woman whose friend holds a rose for her to smell says, "I don't believe in its fragrance" while holding her nose!

The 19th Century noted agnostic, Thomas Huxley, said to a man who was leaving for church on a Sunday morning, "Why don't you stay home and tell me what your faith means to you, and why you are a Christian." The man replied, "Mine is a simple faith—I'm not clever enough to argue with you." Huxley replied, "I don't want to argue with you. I just want you to tell me what Jesus Christ means to you." The man did this. When he had finished there were tears in the famous agnostic's eyes. He said, "I would give my right hand if only I could believe that." He could have demolished the man's arguments or defenses, but the simple "**Come and See**" moved him.

Very few are ever argued into the Kingdom of God. An invitation is better than an argument. My friend, can you say, "I have found the Messiah—He has found me—**Come and See** for yourself." **Come and See** someone who knows all about you and still loves you with an everlasting love. **Come and See** someone who has everything you need—someone who can change your life—someone who has great things for you. Do not turn your back on Jesus and then say, "I don't believe He is the answer."

AFFIRMATION
I will believe and obey
and then enjoy life's greatest sights.

MORE WORDS OF HOPE
"Jesus said to her, 'Did I not tell you that if you
would believe you would see the glory of God?'"
JOHN 11:40

Peace

DECORATION OR DEDICATION

✝

ON MAY 5, 1868, JOHN LOGAN, COMMANDER-IN-CHIEF OF the Grand Army of the Republic, directed that May 30th be set aside "for the purpose of strewing flowers or otherwise decorating the graves of comrades who died in defense of their country." This original Decoration Day is now nationally observed as Memorial Day. It is indeed appropriate that we honor the memory of those who gave their lives for our country.

But to decorate with flowers is not enough. We must dedicate our lives to the Truth that makes men free, to moral rearmament and to the Christian virtues of honesty and love and purity, without which no country can long endure. What I am talking about is recognition of the Sovereignty of God, and our surrender to the rule of Jesus Christ in our lives.

Which is preferable—to decorate the graves of those who died in war, or to work for the prevention of war and the preservation of peace according to God's plan in II Chronicles 7:14? Is our philosophy one of prevention or repair?

Prevention or repair? In our day we spend billions of dollars to *repair* damage to lives because of war, alcohol, sex perversion, drugs, adultery and the like. We spend a bare fraction of this amount on education and on the prevention of human tragedy. We say in effect, "Let's put an ambulance in the valley. After all, it isn't the slipping off the cliff that hurts people—it's the landing at the bottom that bothers us." Thank God for the ambulance. It's a blessing. What a pity that we use it as a substitute for a fence at the edge of the cliff!

We are told that during the initial phases of the construction of the Golden Gate Bridge in San Francisco, no safety devices were used, and 23 men fell to their deaths. A huge net was then installed. Ten men fell into the net and were saved. And 25 percent more work

12

was accomplished when the men were assured of their safety! Christian assurance and our hope for eternity have much to do with our effectiveness and fulfillment as persons in this world!

Decoration or dedication? Do we invest our lives in flowers that fade or in the fullness of the life of Christ that never dies?

AFFIRMATION
Indeed, we remember fallen soldiers, but also
fallen hopes of peace coming through war.

MORE WORDS OF HOPE

"I appeal to you therefore, brethren, by the mercies of God, to present your bodies as a living sacrifice, holy and acceptable to God, which is your spiritual worship. Do not be conformed to this world but be transformed by the renewal of your mind, that you may prove what is the will of God, what is good and acceptable and perfect."
ROMANS 12:1,2

DOING WHAT
YOU CAN'T

✝

AN AMERICAN WAS EXPLAINING TO A FRIEND FROM England the practices of canning fruit. He said, "Of course, we eat most of the fruit we raise on this farm, but what we can't we can." When the Englishman got home he said, "I don't understand those Americans and the way they talk. One told me that they ate what they could and what they couldn't they could."

I recall, as pastor of Augustana Lutheran Church, we made plans to make some 500 calls on sick, shut-in, lapsing, prospective and other friends in a very short period of time. We were reminded of the fact that with God's marching orders He always provides the power to go. It was important to remember that "What we couldn't, we could!"

Many years ago at the Christian Ashram retreat in Northfield, Minnesota, Dr. E. Stanley Jones asked if I would join him in a healing service, in praying and laying on of hands for afflicted persons. I gave an affirmative answer, and shortly thereafter became somewhat panic-stricken with the thought, "What if I block the Spirit's power? What if I am not ready? I can't do it." An hour before the service I told Dr. Jones that I had no freedom to do it. He was great about it and simply said that if at the time of prayers for healing I felt differently that I should come forward.

That night as Dr. Jones spoke of the power of God to heal body and spirit, something happened to me. God put something into me of His faith and love, and power. He made me ready to offer myself as a channel and prayer partner at the altar as many came forward that night. And no one received a greater blessing than I was given! Another reminder that "What I couldn't, I could."

Here is one of the most exciting discoveries in any person's life. When our Lord asks us to witness for Him, to love someone for

Him, to visit, to serve, to suffer and endure for His glory, to do His work in the world, He *always* puts into us His power to do it. Always!

Never say, "I can't." Just open your heart and life to Jesus and He will put into you what it takes to live your life for Him and for others with much abiding fruit. Then your life story can be told in the inscription on the grave stone of a saint of God, "She Hath Done What She Couldn't".

AFFIRMATION
When God says "Go", He also says,
"Lo, I am with you always..."
MATTHEW 28:19,20

MORE WORDS OF HOPE
"I can do all things in him who strengthens me."
PHILIPPIANS 4:13

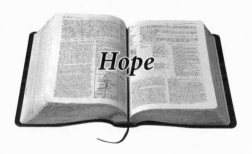

DON'T
BE AFRAID!

✝

A PASTOR ASKED HIS CONGREGATION ONE Sunday morning to read the 17th chapter of St. Mark in preparation for the following Sunday's sermon. Before giving this sermon he asked how many had read Mark 17. Every hand went up. The pastor said, "I have the right audience for my sermon today. It deals with liars. There is no 17th chapter in St. Mark's Gospel." This message is not for liars but for those devastated by fear. For those with fears and apprehensions, the questions is not, "Are you afraid?" but rather, "What are you afraid of?" There is the fear of failure, of losing *independence*, of old age and *dependence*. There is the fear of the future and the unknown. There is the fear of losing home or job. There is the fear of failing health, the fear of cancer and the fear of death. There is the fear of being alone, of being unwanted and unneeded.

What shall we do with fears that devastate both body and spirit? We can lose them in the ultimate fear—the fear without which we cannot be saved. It is the *fear* of God. If fear of God is missing, all of your other fears will take over and devastate your life. Fear of God is, as Dr. Raymond Hedberg has said, "A sober realization of who He is. It is to behold with reverence and awe His greatness and power and love."

I heard a story of two children left alone to care for their five-year-old brother. During a storm the older children cried in fear. The five-year-old brother said, "Stop crying. Don't you suppose God knows His business?"

The little bird sits serenely on the branch lashed by the wind which threatens to cast it down. The bird keeps singing. It has an alternative to destruction. The bird has wings!

Let us not tremble and lament over what the world is coming to. Let us rather rejoice in the first coming of Jesus to this world to redeem it, and in His second coming to rule in glory, with justice and righteousness and peace. And while we wait may we lose our fears in self-giving love and service for Christ and for others.

His eye is on the sparrow and I know he cares for me. (Read Matthew 10:29-31.) Jesus says, "Don't be afraid". He knows His business. He has everything under control.

Affirmation
Fear can be a healthy emotion, but also a block to abundant living. The "fear nots" of the Bible reassure me.

More Words of Hope
*"Fear not, for I am with you, be not dismayed,
for I am your God; I will strengthen you, I will help you,
I will uphold you with my victorious right hand.*
Isaiah 41:10

GOOD NEWS
FOR YOU

✝

HERE IT IS. **YOU CAN BE A GROWING PERSON.** YOU CAN avoid the tragedy of growing older without growing more mature. The late Dr. E. Stanley Jones said, "The consuming illness of our time is our refusal to grow up. Spiritual growth is no longer a luxury for a few. It is a necessity for us all. At the center of almost every acute problem in every area of life is moral and spiritual immaturity." He wrote a book on "Christian Maturity."

This reminds me of a story. It happened in a church at a Sunday evening service. I was walking my six-month-old baby in the rear of the church. He had been crying. A lady came by, looked at the child, looked at me and said, "What a cute baby. Is this your grandson?" I nearly dropped the baby. On the way home, I said to my wife in a complaining voice, "How could she think that I was the grandfather? Do I look that old?" Marta replied, "No, sweetheart, you do not look old. You just look more mature!" Getting older in the Lord should mean that we are getting more mature. May our Lord give us Christian maturity!

An epitaph on a tombstone read, "Here lies John Jones. Died at 40. Buried at 70." He ceased to grow! There was a sign on the door of a college student's room. It read, "If I am studying when you come in, wake me up." Many people are sleeping. They are dying by decay. Someone asked a husband, "Is your wife economical?" He replied, "Well, she had only 26 candles on her 40th birthday cake." How terribly concerned people are about their growing older in years, but so tragically unconcerned about their not growing in creative thought and in spiritual power. A man said, "My mind is already made up. Don't confuse me with the facts." And another sad quotation, "I pray that I might always be right because I never change." Dying by decay—lack of growth!

But here is the Good News. **You can be a growing person**, whether you are 16 or 60 or 90 years old. You can grow in your knowledge of God. You can grow in faith, hope, love, patience. You are made for growth. You can be a creative person. This all sounds good. But how?

Here is a Bible study on spiritual growth. Read the scripture passages carefully. We grow by virtue of being born (John 3:3-5). We grow in union with Jesus Christ. (Galatians 2:20, II Peter 3:18). We grow in His Church. (Ephesians 4:15-16). We grow through obedience. (John 7:17, Exodus 14:15,16). We grow by the power of the Holy Spirit. (Acts 1:8). We grow through suffering. (Philippians 3:10,11). We grow in His Word. (John 8:31,32). We grow in our longing for Home. (II Corinthians 5:1,2). My friend, are you willing to pay the price for spiritual growth?

AFFIRMATION
*If we GROW in the grace and knowledge of our Lord
and Saviour, we will GO and help persons in need.*

MORE WORDS OF HOPE
*"Rather, speaking the truth in love, we are to grow up
in every way into him who is the head, into Christ..."*
EPHESIANS 4:15

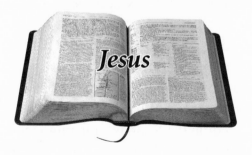

HE DOESN'T SMOKE DURING LENT

✝

A HOLD-UP MAN STUCK HIS GUN IN THE BACK OF A minister and demanded money. When the victim turned around to hand him his wallet, the robber saw the clerical collar, pulled his gun away and said apologetically, "I'm sorry, I never take money from the clergy." The minister was so relieved and so confused that he said, "Oh, you need not apologize, here have a cigar." The hold-up man replied, "No thanks, I don't smoke during Lent."

This is the attitude of many persons concerning Lent; namely, to give up something to gain merit before God. Quite often it is something they should not have or something they should not be doing at all. What will it take to get smokers to give up cigarettes? Will it take death from lung cancer? Will it take the rude jolt of hypocrisy that laments pollution while engaging in one of our most serious pollution problems? Will it take a Lenten ritual? Or will it take a new relationship to Jesus Christ? What will it take to get us to give up spending overtime in the wasteland of television? What will it take to get many to give up the drinking that contributes to America's number one drug problem today? What will it take to get us to give up overeating which is a major sin indeed? Or to give up the sin of gossip? Or the sin of greed?

What will it take to get you to include in your daily schedule time for God's Word and prayer? What will it take to get you to include in your weekly schedule the Sunday morning worship hour?

This I know, that it will take more than a Lenten practice or the pleading of a preacher. It will take a face-to-face meeting with the Christ of the Word and of the Cross. If the love of the suffering Servant of God going to the cross to die for sinners like you and me cannot constrain us to give up something for Him, then what could possibly do it?

The Lenten season is not only the time to give up something. It is the time to **give up something in order to take up more of what we need from our Lord**! Give your sin and guilt to Him, your sorrow and failures and regrets. Then take His Word and Promise in Isaiah 53:4-6.

AFFIRMATION
*I want to give up something in order to
have more to give to others in need.*

MORE WORDS OF HOPE
*"He who did not spare his own Son but gave him up for
us all, will he not also give us all things with him?"*
ROMANS 8:32

TO WHOM ARE YOU LISTENING?

✝

DID YOU EVER SAY TO SOMEONE, "NOW, YOU LISTEN TO me!" If you have to press someone to listen to you—to beg them or threaten them—then you must not have anything helpful to say. "Pay attention to me—I'm the authority—I know the way." It's not very convincing. You become a burden rather than a blessing. I recall a cartoon in which a mother is sitting in the back seat of a "just married" car, telling her daughter, the bride, and her son-in-law how to spend their honeymoon. She had never learned about the Listening Post.

Listening Post? Yes, the place of prayer. The place of looking up (Psalm 121). The place of renewal (Isaiah 40:28,31). The place of release from fear (Isaiah 12:2). The place of guidance (Psalm 32:8).

Prayer is not overcoming God's reluctance, saying, "Listen to me." It is taking hold of God's highest willingness. He wills the Best for us.

My friend, do you pray selfishly in the spirit of "Listen to me and give me what I want." A little boy was asked if he prayed every day. He said, "No, not every day. Some days I don't want anything."

Prayer is not an easy way of getting what we want, but the only way of becoming what God wants us to be.

Prayer is not self-assertion. It is self-surrender. True prayer exalts Jesus Christ. In prayer we acknowledge God's Power and glory, and His Lordship in our lives. I can be an incredible optimist because of who God is, and because of what I know He can do.

Listen! He is saying, "Come to me—I will give you rest." And more. He offers strength and help for daily life. Listen and respond with praise as you read Ephesians 3:20,21.

AFFIRMATION
Someone has said, "A coffee break is good."
A prayer break is better. A listening break is
even better and a praise break is the best.

MORE WORDS OF HOPE
"And a cloud overshadowed them, and a voice came
out of the cloud, 'This is my beloved Son; listen to him.'"
Mark 9:7

HOW DO YOU PRAY?

✝

DURING A VISIT TO A CARE CENTER, A 92-YEAR-OLD WOMAN stopped me and said, "Pastor Berg, did you hear about the single young man who longed for love and marriage? He did not want to ask God for such a big favor for himself so he prayed the following prayer, 'Dear Lord, I don't ask anything for myself but would you please send my mother a daughter-in-law?'"

This is the way many people pray. They camouflage their self-interest by apparent concern for others. One lady prayed, "Dear Lord, please help my sister-in-law to change so I can love her."

Prayer is not for the purpose of getting something for ourselves. Prayer is not for the purpose of getting out of fox holes or tight places. Prayer is primarily for the purpose of glorifying God, of recognizing who He is and who we are—sinners completely dependent on Him. Prayer is essentially *surrender*—"not my will, but thine be done". It is *trust* as we place our lives in Jesus' hands. Prayer is a *relationship* out of which comes praise and adoration and *obedience*.

Prayer is no substitute for obedience. A little girl seeing the gardener place traps in her garden to catch the birds that were her friends prayed, "Please God, don't let the birds come near the traps. And God, if they do, please don't let the traps work." Then she thought about it for awhile and went out and kicked the traps to pieces!

In Exodus 14:15, we find Moses crying to God to deliver His people. "The Lord said to Moses, 'Why do you cry to me? Tell the people to go forward.'" In prayer we stop, look and listen. We receive guidelines and marching orders. Then we rise and go. We become the answer—His **delivered children**.

THE PRAYER OF AN UNKNOWN CONFEDERATE SOLDIER

I asked God for strength, that I might achieve.

I was made weak, that I might learn humbly to obey.

I asked for health, that I might do greater things.

I was given infirmity, that I might do better things.

I asked for riches, that I might be happy.

I was given poverty, that I might be wise.

I asked for power that I might have the praise of men.

I was given weakness that I might feel the need of God.

I asked for all things, that I might enjoy life.

I was given life, that I might enjoy all things.

I got nothing that I asked for—but everything I hoped for.

Almost despite myself, my unspoken prayers were answered
I am, among all men, most richly blessed.

AFFIRMATION
Prayer does not change things
but changes and transforms me.

MORE WORDS OF HOPE
"For I know the plans I have for you, says the Lord,
plans for welfare and not for evil, to give you a future
and a hope. Then you will call upon me and come
and pray to me, and I will hear you. You will seek
me and find me; when you seek me with all your heart."
JEREMIAH 29:11-13

HOW MANY
MINISTERS IN THE
WORLD

✝

GOD OFFERS HIS GIFTS TO EACH MEMBER OF THE BODY. There are no exceptions. Each person joined to Jesus Christ by faith, and indwelt by His Spirit, has special gifts to be used in a healing and reconciling ministry for God and for others.

Dr. George Washington Carver, world-renowned scientist, educator and leader, was asked how he got started in his scientific discoveries. He replied, "I put a peanut in my open hand and said, 'Mr. Creator, what's in that peanut?' The Creator answered, 'You have brains. Go and find out.'" He did find out. He developed 300 products from the peanut and over 100 from the sweet potato, primarily to develop agriculture in the South and for the uplift of humanity. Here was a humble man, called to be a minister of Christ, called to build up the Body of Christ.

A humble, committed pastor was criticized by many in his congregation for being a poor preacher, an inadequate youth leader, and for other things. The pastor's young son became ill with what doctors said was a terminal illness. Now the father knew that his son had received Jesus as His Saviour, and that death would be his entrance into heaven. But he pondered the question, "How do you tell a lively young boy who loves life that he is going to die in a few days?" The father prayed for divine guidance. He shared God's promises with his son and prayed with him. Then he said, "Are you afraid, my son, to meet Jesus?" Blinking away a few tears , the boy replied, "No, not if He's like you, dad." The father was not a great preacher or leader, but he was a **great minister** of God, truly great in the glory of Jesus and His love.

There is no doubt in my mind that among the truly great ministers in this world are the unheralded saints of God, the shut-in and infirm—older persons who sense their high calling to care and to pray—those whose lives affirm the Good News that God's Grace is always sufficient.

You are called to be a minister of Christ. Congratulations!

Affirmation
We are called to be more than ministers,
ministering to others, we are called to be reconcilers.
II Corinthians 5:18, 19

More Words of Hope
"You did not choose me, but I chose you and appointed
you that you should go and bear fruit and that your
fruit should abide; so that whatever you ask the Father
in my name, he may give it to you."
John 15:16

HOW TO
BE SAVED

†

THE BIBLE SAYS, "BELIEVE IN THE LORD JESUS, AND YOU
will be saved, you and your household." Acts 16:31. Again we read in
Romans 10:9, "If you confess with your lips that Jesus is Lord and
believe in your heart that God raised him from the dead, you will be
saved." Giving lip service only is a sure way to be lost. Jesus tells us
in Matthew 7:21, "Not everyone who says to me, 'Lord, Lord', shall
enter the kingdom of heaven, but he who does the will of my Father
who is in heaven."

Among the most persuasive "evangelists" of our day are the radio
and television personalities who tell people how to be saved. Saved
from what? Here are some examples: "Save me from tooth decay—
give me Crest. Save me from insecurity—give me a bank account.
Save me from dishwater hands—give me Palmolive. Save me from
romance that fades—give me a better deodorant. Save me from
tasteless meals—give me Hamburger Helper. Save me from communism—give me weapons of war. Save me from filtered-out flavor—
give me a real cigarette. Save me from economic depression—give
me more money to spend and to waste." This is what salvation
means to many people.

Salvation, the real thing, means being saved from the sins that
destroy body and soul rather than being cast into eternal darkness
and separation from God. This means being saved from sin and
death and the power of the devil. It means being saved from God's
judgment and wrath. It means being saved from a form of godliness
without power. Yes, and it means being saved from the madness of
militarism and from the crippling effects of racial discrimination. It
means being saved from the devastating effects of unresolved guilt.

But being saved means more than rescue from danger and
destruction. It means being saved **for a new life of service for**

Christ and for others. Salvation means believing in Jesus, and **doing** the will of our Father in Heaven. Martin Luther said, "Believing in Christ as your Saviour means being a Christ to your neighbor."

The way to be lost is to have creeds without deeds—to name the Name without knowing Him—to engage in activity for Christ without commitment to Him.

How to be saved. Believe in God and *act* upon His will. Trust and obey!

AFFIRMATION
Faith means more than believing with the mind.
It means obeying the commandments of God.

MORE WORDS OF HOPE
"And this is his commandment, that we should believe
in the name of his Son Jesus Christ and love one another,
just as he has commanded us."
I JOHN 3:23

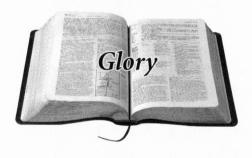

I BELIEVE
IN MIRACLES!

✝

JOHN, A YOUNG ARMY RECRUIT, WAS SAYING A FOND farewell to his fiancee, Mary, just before boarding a ship for a year of service overseas. Amidst their tears and embraces, the girl slipped a ring from her finger. Putting it on one of his fingers she said, "Please wear this ring. When you see it you will see me—when you feel the ring you will be touching me. And promise me that you will never remove this ring from your finger until you put it back on my finger." He promised and during his year abroad the ring proved to be a great source of comfort to the young man. His daily letters told of the significance of that symbol and how grateful he was for it and how it helped him survive.

A year later as he was returning to the New York harbor he stood on the bridge of the ship reflecting on what a life-saver that ring had been. In just seven days he could slip it on his sweetheart's finger again. In his emotional reverie he broke his promise and removed the ring from his finger. Suddenly the ring slipped from his grasp into the ocean. He was shocked! How could he face her without the ring?

A week later, just before leaving the city for his fiancee's home, he went to a restaurant and ordered fresh fish for dinner. During the meal he felt a hard object in his mouth. He removed the object and held in his fingers—a fish bone!

Did some of you think that the hard object was the ring? You must believe in miracles! Greater miracles than this happen. This would be a small miracle for our Lord. He made it possible for Simon Peter to find a sheckel in the mouth of a fish so he could pay his taxes. He turned water into wine. He healed the sick and raised the dead. I do not believe in Jesus Christ because of His miracles. I believe in the miracles because of Jesus Christ! I do not believe in Jesus because of His Virgin Birth. I believe in the Virgin Birth because of Jesus Christ! His life is a miracle and He made the marriage of John and Mary His miracle of union—Christian marriage. A miracle indeed.

Take away the miracles and you take away Christ. And mark this—miracles do not abrogate or suspend the laws of nature. They happen because of a new power that is introduced. A boy throws a ball in the air. The fact that the ball goes up for a moment does not suspend the law of gravity. There is a new force—the muscular power of the boy and the act of his will, that must be taken into consideration.

Your life also can be a miracle, a miracle of faith and hope and love centered in Jesus, our Saviour and Lord.

Affirmation
Jesus turned disease into health and blindness into
sight, and he can transform us sinners into saints.

More Words of Hope
"Therefore, if any one is in Christ, he is a new creation;
the old has passed away, behold, the new has come."
II Corinthians 5:17

INCREDIBLE
OPTIMISM
✝

PONDER FOR A MOMENT THE INCREDIBLE OPTIMISM OF Jesus, who says in John 10:27-29, "My sheep recognize my voice, and I know them, and they follow me; no one shall snatch them out of my hand. My father, who has given them to me, is greater than all, and no one is able to snatch them out of the Father's hand." This is blessed assurance for all who surrender to God's love, and who are willing to be born again into a new life in Jesus through faith and obedience.

An optimistic revolutionary says, "We'll overthrow the government and be free." The pessimistic revolutionary says, "But after we overthrow the government, where will we get our welfare checks?" A bishop lamented, "Wherever St. Paul went there was a revolution. Wherever I go they serve tea." We are indeed involved in a revolution. We are called to action—God's action in creating new birth in persons and new structures for peace and freedom and justice in the world. Building upon Jesus Christ, the Son of the Living God and the only Saviour, the gates of hell shall not prevail against this revolution.

I like the optimism of a little boy who was cheering on the sidelines of a baseball game. A stranger came along and asked him how the game was going. The boy replied, "Wonderful." "What's the score?" the man asked. "It's 33 to nothing" came the reply. The man responded, "No wonder that you are cheering with a lead like that." But when the man heard that they were *behind* 33 to nothing he said, "How come you are cheering like this. Aren't you discouraged?" The boy replied, "Discouraged? Why man, we ain't come to bat yet!"

I read recently a story about John Philip Sousa, the world-famous musician, and author of the spirited march, "The Stars and Stripes Forever". Sitting in his hotel room one summer evening, Mr. Sousa heard an organ grinder in the street below playing his march in a slow, dragging manner. He dashed down to the street and called to the sleepy organ-grinder, "That's no way to play that march!" He seized the handle of the organ and turned it vigorously. The music rushed out, spirited and snappy. The organ man bowed low and smiled. The next night Mr. Sousa heard the organ again. This time the tempo was right. Looking out of his hotel window he saw a great crowd gathering about the organ player. Over the organ on a large placard was the organ-grinder's name. Under the name in larger letters were these words, **"Pupil of John Philip Sousa".**

It must be God's incredible optimism that calls us to be His pupils and co-workers. My optimism is rooted in the words of Jesus Who said, "You did not choose me, but I chose you and appointed you that you should go and bear fruit and that your fruit should abide..." John 15:16.

Affirmation
*What incredible optimism God reveals in His divine
plan to transform us rescued sinners into saints.*

More Words of Hope
*"I have said this to you, that in me you may have peace.
In the world you have tribulation; but be of good cheer,
I have overcome the world."*
John 16:33

IT RAINED AT HIROSHIMA

✝

ON OCTOBER 16, 1978, MEMBERS OF OUR CHRISTIAN
Ashram group stood at the Peace Monument in Hiroshima, Japan.
We were a sober and silent group. The rain was falling. On August
6, 1945, it rained an ominous black rain that contained huge doses
of lethal radio-activity. Seventy thousand persons were killed with
tens of thousands dying later as a result of the atomic holocaust. We
stood there with Pastor Tanimoto. His church was destroyed in
1945, and many of his people killed. He was miraculously spared to
become one of the heroes of the rescue operation. Pastor Tanimoto
is one of the main characters in the book, "Hiroshima". His church
is engaged in many post-war redemptive ministries.

It was my privilege and awesome responsibility to lead the worship service for our group at the Peace Monument. We prayed
together, "Lord, have mercy upon us; Lord, have mercy upon Japan;
Lord, have mercy upon the United States; Lord, have mercy upon
your Church." We shared this word from I Chronicles 28:20: "If my
people, who are called by my name, shall humble themselves and
pray, and seek my face, and turn from their wicked ways, then will I
hear from heaven, and will forgive their sin, and heal their land." It
was an emotional experience. We stood under divine judgment.
Then we moved to stand under divine grace. I shared the story of
the Japanese girl, terribly burned and disfigured in the holocaust,
who with some 25 others, came to the United States for surgery.
This girl was surrounded by Christian love. Still disfigured, and on
the way to her thirteenth plastic surgery operation, she said to an
attendant, "Please tell Dr. Barsky for me that he should not feel so
bad because he cannot give me a new face. Tell him that I have
received a new heart and that everything is ok." Bless her. She was at
peace and was helping to build a peace monument.

What's the answer? More and more violence, war and killing as we are witnessing in many nations today? No, but rather the violence of an earthquake at Calvary, the veil of the temple rent asunder, the rain pouring down after Jesus died on the cross, reminding us of the blood of the Lamb flowing into lives to create new hearts. It's the only way for survival!

In Pastor Tanimoto's church, we sensed deeply a rebirth, rising out of the ashes and desolation—a Redemption Center. As the great choir sang, I caught a vision of the indestructible Church, strong enough to batter down the gates of Hell rising up to destroy it.

AFFIRMATION
*I thank God for His unshakable kingdom
and the unchanging person, Jesus.*

MORE WORDS OF HOPE
*"Therefore let us be grateful for receiving a kingdom
that cannot be shaken, and thus let us offer to God
acceptable worship, with reverence and awe."*
HEBREWS 12:28

LET'S GET AWAY— WHAT FOR?

✝

RECENTLY I RECEIVED AN UNSIGNED LETTER IN WHICH THE writer indicated that I was doing a very poor job. I do not receive such strong sentiments often, perhaps not as often as I deserve.

The writer of this letter indicated that we were glorying in statistics, on an ego trip, riding on the backs of people in need to get a reputation as "do-gooders", and that we should not draw attention to ourselves. Well, I have often said that in our Crossroad and Community Emergency Service ministries, we face the risk of appearing as benefactors and of calling attention to our goodness. Not only is it a risk, but often a reality which reminds us of our human weakness and fallibility. I deeply believe that Jesus Christ must be the Center of all ministries. If He is not lifted up we pull people down. Our deepest desire is to point to Him as the source of all that is good and to help people Meet the Master whose love encompasses all physical and spiritual needs. The divine incentives for God's work in His Church must be found in John 3:16 and I John 3:16. Please pray that in the midst of human weakness His word will cleanse our attitudes and guide our ways.

The disciples of Jesus returned one day from a missionary journey. They must have been excited. They told Jesus about what they had done and taught. The focus was upon them. Jesus knew that they needed to get their evaluations and perspectives in order. He said, "Come apart and rest." Read the story in Mark 6:30-34. In other words, let's get away from the crowd—*and from ourselves!* Now many think if they can only get away to the cabin, to the vacation place, to the change of schedule, to some different or exciting place, that they will be renewed. The secret of renewal is not in getting away, *but in getting away with Jesus* and of having a time exposure to His person and teaching.

A golfer often asked his neighbor to play golf with him. One Sunday morning on the golf course he said, "I have asked you dozens of times to go with me to the golf course. But I cannot remember that you ever asked me to come to your church with you." For this church member, getting away meant getting away from God and from his Christian responsibilities.

I recall my Mother's words to me following a glowing report I gave her on an Evangelism Mission, "Were any souls saved?" It's good for us to review our motives and incentives and emphases. What is all the activity in the Church about? We hope that it's about Jesus Christ!

AFFIRMATION
Our choice is: Come apart with Jesus or
come apart—meditation or medication.

MORE WORDS OF HOPE
"Come to me, all who labor and are heavy laden, and I will give you rest. Take my yoke upon you, and learn from me; for I am gentle and lowly in heart, and you will find rest for your souls. For my yoke is easy, and my burden is light.
MATTHEW 11:28-30

LITTLE LEAGUERS
AND BIG LEAGUERS

I SAW A CARTOON THE OTHER DAY THAT FEATURED A Little Leaguer, a child in baseball uniform. However, he was not playing baseball. The little fellow was carrying a placard that read, "On Strike." His coach, looking at the little boy, said to the assistant coach, "It all started when I told my Little Leaguers to act like Big Leaguers."

The lesson? Well, let's ask ourselves, "What kind of an example am I to a little child? If he follows me, will he go right or wrong? Do I inspire him to grasp for more and more of material things instead of reaching for higher values? Am I leading someone toward heaven or hell?

I recall, as a Little League coach in New Jersey several years ago, that **parents** were often booing the umpire, griping and setting a horrible example for the youngsters who always played a fine and clean-cut game.

Would you like to have a little child, perhaps your own, follow in your footsteps? I recall one of my children, when very small, saying, "Daddy, I'm going to do whatever you do." What a challenge! What a responsibility!

St. Paul writes in I Corinthians 8:12, "Thus, sinning against your brethren and wounding their conscience when it is weak, you sin against Christ."

Speaking of our life example, what kind of memories will we leave behind for loved ones and friends when we have departed from this world? Will they remember us as persons who lived out our Christian faith in daily life as died-for, forgiven and committed followers of Christ in whom His love was seen and felt? What will you be doing when God summons you? Martin Luther, when asked what he would do if this was his last day on earth replied, "I'd plant a tree." Will your loved ones and friends be able to celebrate Life and Hope in the midst of death at your memorial service?

Little Leaguers follow Big Leaguers. Children follow parents. The weak follow the strong. We are called to follow Jesus Christ and to be made into His Likeness. It's the only safe and satisfying way!

AFFIRMATION
I will be a good example if I follow in Jesus' steps
and a dangerous one if I go my own way.

MORE WORDS OF HOPE
"Let your light so shine before men, that they may see your good works and give glory to your Father who is in heaven."
MATTHEW 5:16

NO ONE
DOES IT BETTER

✝

IN FACT, NO ONE CAN DO IT AS WELL, WHETHER IT IS healing of the body and spirit, feeding the hungry, providing justice and freedom for all people, reclaiming wasted lives, educating the mind, disciplining the will, teaching people the meaning of love and how to love redemptively, healing broken relationships—no one can even approach the better plan of Jesus Christ.

Some of us who are older will recall the television series entitled "Ozzie and Harriet". I recall one of the episodes telling of Walter coming to visit his friend Ricky, and parents, Ozzie and Harriet Nelson. Ozzie played football, carved the turkey, told a bedtime story, engaged in lawn acrobatics and really did an impressive job of showing himself to be as wonderful as Ricky had advertised his father to be. But after every valiant effort, Walter, aged 9, would say, "You sure do a great job, Mr. Nelson, but, of course, not as good as my dad. No one in the world can do it as good as he can." A slow burn of resentment was building up in Ozzie. In fact, he was glad when Walter's mother came to take him home. An attractive young lady, she said to Ozzie, "I'm so glad to meet you. Ricky has been telling me what a wonderful father he has." Ozzie replied, "As a matter of fact, I've been very eager to meet you, yes, and especially Walter's father. From what Walter tells me he must really be a great guy." "We think so," replied Walter's mother. Then with tears in her eyes she continued, "You see Walter has never seen his father. He died on Corrigidor when our son was a baby."

Walter had a beautiful obsession about his father whom he had never seen. To him, he was the greatest. No one could do it better. My friend, how do you feel about Jesus whom you have seen dying on a Cross for you? Do you really believe that He does everything better—that He has the Best of everything for you?

Bishop James K. Mathews, prominent leader in the Methodist Church and leader of the Christian Ashram movement in many countries, always signed off on our telephone visits with these words, "All the best".

"The best" will include the "alls" of Romans 8:28 and 8:32.

AFFIRMATION
God provided the Best for His lost son returning home-
the best robe and the fatted calf for the banquet.
LUKE 15:22-23

MORE WORDS OF HOPE
"But as it is, Christ has obtained a ministry which is as
much more excellent than the old as the covenant he
mediates is better, since it is enacted on better promises."
HEBREWS 8:6

PENTECOST AND HUMAN RIGHTS

✝

IN OUR DAY A MAJOR AND BURNING ISSUE IS THAT OF human rights. Few people comprehend either the term or the concept. Human rights, to be understood, must be placed in proper perspective with "divine rights". God created every person in His own image. When each one of us got lost in the fall of the human race, our Lord redeemed us, bought us back by the atoning death of His Son on the cross. Pentecost affirms and guarantees the divine destiny of each person as the Holy Spirit comes to indwell us. This means **Christ in us**—His presence and power and perfection! Without an adequate self-image made possible by our Lord's acceptance of us and by His invasion of our lives, the human rights movement is shallow and meaningless.

In our day we hear much about "the right to do as you please". This includes the right to defy God's moral law which really means contempt for all law. It is a crusade for the right to live at your own human, degraded level, no matter who is hurt or destroyed. This perspective of life keeps you from being the better person you ought to be and could be under Divine Power.

The question, "Whatever became of human rights?" must never be separated from the question, "Whatever became of sin?" the sin of flaunting our humanity—sin that separates persons from the source of all that is good and just and true.

Let's face the reality and power of sin which demeans and destroys people. Are you willing to confess your sins which deprive you and others of your "divine rights"?

Four pastors decided to open up to each other and to confess secret sins. One said, "I love wild west movies and skip meetings at church to watch these shows." Another said, "I'm addicted to cigarettes and am risking my health". The third pastor said, "I'm a gambler". The fourth man was silent, but when pressed to confess, he said, "My sin is gossip, and I can hardly wait to get out of here"!

What is the sin that you should confess and be rid of?

AFFIRMATION
The gift of the Holy Spirit can make me the
message of new life and hope for others.

MORE WORDS OF HOPE
"For God took the sinless Christ and poured into him our sins.
Then, in exchange, he poured God's goodness into us."
II CORINTHIANS 5:21 (LB)

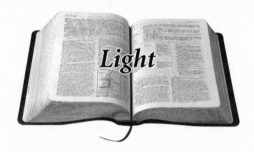

SIGNS OF THE KINGDOM—IN RUSSIA

STRANGELY ENOUGH, IT WAS IN ATHEISTIC RUSSIA—IN Leningrad that the sign of our Lord's Unshakable Kingdom was dramatized most impressively for me. During one visit in 1979, I saw a monument in "Bloody Square". On the top was a Cross with an angel pointing to it. I thought, "Hard as they try, they cannot get rid of Love and Truth." You cannot destroy the Cross. You cannot avoid it—Russia was still under the Cross—the Cross of divine judgment and divine love. Someone has said, "Hammar away, ye hostile hands. Your hammars break—God's anvil stands."

In the Hermitage Museum of Art in Leningrad, I saw the world-famous Michelangelo collection of 26 original paintings. The most impressive were "The Descent From the Cross" and "The Return of the Prodigal". The Marxist Communists tried to root out religion and God and His truth. To do this they would have been forced to destroy the finest in art and literature and music. That Cross and these paintings in Leningrad reminded me of the Unshakable Kingdom.

The Kingdom of communism is shakable. They held it together by force—by purges and walls. Without the human props it fell apart. The Kingdom of capitalism is shakable. The stock market fluctuates with a president's heartbeat or with his temperament. The Kingdom of self is shakable. It is destined to go to pieces. The Kingdom of wealth is shakable. The Kingdom of military might is shakable. Witness what happened in Nazi Germany and to militaristic Japan.

Did you know that Aaron Burr, the American leader accused of treason, was once within **one vote** of the Presidency of the United States? Here is his tragic story. A spiritual awakening was taking place on the campus of Princeton University. Aaron Burr felt led to surrender his life to Christ. But the University president advised him to "Cool it—get your emotions under control". So Aaron Burr indeed cooled off. He said, "Jesus, if you will now leave me alone, I'll promise to leave you alone." He sought his own kingdom of self and earthly power. He killed Alexander Hamilton in a dual. He became a man without a country. He tried to destroy the country he could have served as President. All this because he rejected the Kingdom—Christ's rule within his heart.

My friend, is it the Kingdom of self or the Kingdom of God for you? Are you attached by faith and by a personal surrender of your life to Jesus Christ—attached to the Unshakable Kingdom and to the Unchanging Person?

AFFIRMATION
To be obsessed with the unshakable kingdom
and the unchanging person is a magnificent
obsession for which I am eternally grateful.

MORE WORDS OF HOPE
"But seek first his kingdom and his righteousness,
and all these things shall be yours as well."
MATTHEW 6:33

SILENT NIGHT— HUNGRY NIGHT

☩

LET ME SHARE WITH YOU ANOTHER VERSION OF THE Christmas carol, "Silent Night", as we seek to bring the Nativity Scene into the midst of our broken, sin-sick world.

> Silent night—hungry night,
>   Starving, dying—what a sight!
> Round yon virgin the children lie,
>   Mary's baby came also to die.
>
> Outstretched hands cast a pall,
>   Behold the Cross on the wall.
> Silent night—hungry night,
>   Sorrow, sickness—there's a light!
>
> Healing rays from His holy face,
>   Multitudes freed by redeeming grace.
> Jesus, my Lord, at your birth,
>   Jesus, my Lord, at your Cross.

Yes, I see on that dimly lit stable wall the shadow of His Cross. I hear the prophet's voice from long ago, "He was wounded for our transgressions. . . with His stripes we are healed."

In the shadow of that Cross I see emaciated and starving children. I hear mothers crying as they watch their children die in their arms. Silent night—hungry night. They are hungry for food. They are hungry for freedom and for home. I see refugees in despair, waiting for someone to care—hungry for a home. I see lonely persons missing loved ones who have gone before. I see the afflicted ones, the depressed, friends in pain, fear and insecurity. Silent night—hungry night. They are hungry for healing—healing of body and spirit, healing of the emotions and the memories.

46

My friend, will you come to the manger and the Cross? Will you bring your sins to the Savior? Will you bring your heart for cleansing and your life offered for His service? Will you bring your gifts for the hungry and love for others—His love in you?

Then hungry night becomes Holy Night. Hallelujah!

AFFIRMATION
Giving gifts to hungry and starving persons
means giving gifts to Jesus.
MATTHEW 25:40.

MORE WORDS OF HOPE
"And the King will answer them, 'Truly,
I say to you, as you did it to one of the least
of these my brethren, you did it to me.'"
MATTHEW 25:40

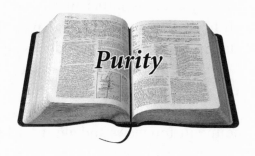

Purity

SOME THOUGHTS FROM MOUNTAIN TOPS

✝

MANY YEARS AGO, AT A RETREAT AT BETHEL SEMINARY IN ST. Paul, I climbed a hill located on that beautiful rolling and wooded campus. As I was climbing I received new strength in the words of the song, "We Are Climbing Jacob's Ladder". At the top I caught an expansive view of the countryside. Then I reflected, "God can see the expanse of my future. He has the complete panorama of plans for me." I caught a new vision of God in my future. Jesus' words came clearly to me, "My Grace is sufficient for you".

Then I was ready to go down from this high place. Walking down, I sang two extra stanzas of the "Jacob's Ladder" song—words that I made up on the way: "We are ready for the valley—Soldier of the Cross. Jesus' grace is all-sufficient—Soldier of the Cross".

I believe that God is never more real, never closer, than in the valley. He gives us mountain-top views and glimpses, but I believe His power and glory are mightily revealed in the valley of human need and brokenness.

During another mountain-top experience I had a special meeting with my Lord. It happened in the prayer vigil room at an Ashram on the Carlton College campus in Northfield. I had been seeking divine guidance for several weeks regarding the call to serve as pastor of Augustana Lutheran Church in Minneapolis. In that hour I received blessed assurance and release from God. I knew for sure that my Lord had chosen me and that He was sending me into this ministry. With that deep sense of being chosen and sent, I could carry the burdens and the storms, the pressures and blessings, the risks and challenges. And the Lord has been very real and completely sufficient for every need and circumstance.

On a church parking lot on a Sunday evening I had another mountain-top experience. Pastor Walter Battle and his radio quartet gave a rousing, hand-clapping, shouting, praise-filled program. At the close I put my arm around Brother Battle and said, "We Lutherans and Pentecostals really get along fine together". Indeed, we are partners in ministry, serving our Lord and Saviour and others in His name.

AFFIRMATION
I'm grateful for mountain top experiences, but I breathe more freely in the valley of human need.

MORE WORDS OF HOPE
"Even though I walk through the valley of the shadow of death, I fear no evil; for thou art with me; thy rod and thy staff, they comfort me."
PSALM 23:4

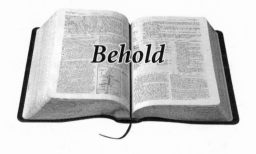

SOMETHING GOOD IS GOING TO HAPPEN TO YOU

✝

IT'S MORE THAN A SENTIMENTAL SONG—MORE THAN singing in the dark. It's more than wishful thinking and shallow optimism.Someone has said, "Optimism is what the teakettle has. Up to its neck in hot water, it keeps on singing." Another definition: "An optimist is one who makes the best of it when he gets the worst of it." There's not much depth in these definitions. I like this one: "Optimism is the consciousness of hidden reserves."

Here is a picture of ultimate optimism from Luke's Gospel: An old man, Simeon, had been waiting a long time for the coming of the Messiah. We read in Luke 2:26(TLB), "For the Holy Spirit had revealed to him that he would not die until he had seen him—God's anointed King." Simeon knew that something good was going to happen. The basis of his optimism was God's Word and promise. This is far different from contrived optimism centered in circumstances and feelings.

Something good did happen to Simeon. He saw the Saviour in Mary and Joseph's baby. "Lord," he said, "now I can die content!. . . I have seen the Savior. . ." Luke 2:29-30(TLB).

His optimism was more than "possibility thinking". It was related to "optimus", meaning the *best*. He was waiting for the Best and saw it in the face of Jesus Christ. Enthusiasm comes from en theos, meaning *in God*. This is *anchored* and *ultimate* optimism.

Yes, and Simeon's optimism was rational and realistic. He turned to Mary in the midst of his ecstasy and said, "A sword shall pierce your soul, for this child shall be rejected by many. . ." Luke 2:35(TLB). Wise old Simeon! He puts humanists and success addicts to shame. He was aware of the reality of sin—of an infected and fallen race. That's what the coming of the Messiah was all about. One cannot be an authentic optimist without an awareness of the sword, the violence, the broken relationships, the struggles for liberation or without claiming *salvation from sin* and the *Grace that is greater than our guilt.*

Christian optimism includes the right to fail and the possibility of defeat. Simeon knew that the Messiah would specialize in such problems and provide the cure. Thank God for the magnificent realism of the Gospel—the full gospel of sin and grace, of defeat and victory, of dying and coming alive.

AFFIRMATION
Optimism based on eternal truth is a priceless gift.

MORE WORDS OF HOPE
"For this gospel I was appointed a preacher and apolstle and teacher, and therefore I suffer as I do. But I am not ashamed, for I know whom I have believed, and I am sure that he is able to guard until that Day what has been entrusted to me."
II TIMOTHY 1:11,12

SPEAKING OF INTRODUCTIONS

✝

THE TOASTMASTER AT A BANQUET WAS INTRODUCING THE main speaker. He said with grand eloquence, "Our speaker tonight is one of the best known men in this area. His name is upon every lip. His name is a by-word and an inspiration. I proudly present to you Mr....Mr....ah...Sorry, I've forgotten your name."

When I first came to my former parish in Rock Island, Illinois, a business man was introducing me to his friend. He said, "Rev. Berg here has come to be pastor of one of the greatest churches in our city. His church is widely known. That church has made its mark in this community. It's the...the...say, Reverend, what is the name of your church?"

Or take the example of the man who introduced the banquet speaker as follows: "Ladies and Gentlemen, I present to you our speaker, Mr. Johnson. He is from Idaho. He made $50,000 in potatoes." The speaker arose and said, "Thank you, Mr. Chairman, but I must make a slight correction. My name is not Johnson. It is Peterson. I am not from Idaho. I am from Texas. I do not deal in potatoes. I deal in oil. I did not make $50,000. I lost it. Oh yes, also, it was not me. It was my brother! Otherwise your introduction was substantially correct."

Now, my friend, if you were asked to introduce Jesus to someone, could you do it correctly? What would you say? Would you get it all mixed up? Would you leave out the most important part? Would you say that He is the best man who ever lived on earth? Perhaps you would say that He is the greatest teacher—that He is a healer and miracle worker, the beautiful Saviour, King of Creation. This is good, but not good enough. You would have to give more information. The only way to do this is to **know** Him **personally**.

Would you be able to introduce Jesus by using the words of the explanation of the Second Article of the Apostles' Creed, "He's my

Lord, who has redeemed me, a lost and condemned creature. He has bought me and freed me from all sin, from death and from the power of the devil."

Perhaps we can learn from the little boy who was converted and went around introducing Jesus like this, "Jesus! He's wonderful! He took the rap for me!"

AFFIRMATION
I'm grateful that Jesus introduces Himself to me
in His Word so I can introduce Him to others.

MORE WORDS OF HOPE
"Greater love has no man than this, that a man
lay down his life for his friends. You are my
friends if you do what I command you."
JOHN 15:13,14

STEEPLE
OR PEOPLE!

✝

MANY YEARS AGO, I VISITED THE MÜNSTER CHURCH IN Germany. This magnificent and imposing cathedral has the highest church steeple in the world—537 feet. Friends challenged me to climb with them to the top—768 steps. Given more time in that city I think I would have made the climb. The reward would have been a spectacular view.

Instead, we focused on people and on each other as we prayed together in the church. We spoke of loved ones and friends. We touched people by way of intercession. In other words, we gave up the *panoramic view* for the *personal touch*.

More emphasis ought to be placed on person-to-person relationships. To be Christ-centered is to be **person-centered**, with concern for persons for whom He died.

Speaking of the panoramic view versus the personal touch reminds me of this poem:

THE PARISH PRIEST OF AUSTERITY
By Brewer Mattocks

The parish priest of austerity
   Climbed up in a high church steeple,
To be nearer God so that he might hand
   His word down to the people.
And in sermon script, he daily wrote,
   What he thought was sent from heaven,
And dropped this down on the people's heads
   Two times, one day in seven.
In his age God said, "Come down and die,"
   And he cried out from the steeple,
"Where art Thou, Lord?" And the Lord replied,
   "Down here among my people."

54

Let us be grateful for church steeples with the cross on top. Above all, let us be grateful that Jesus came down to lift us sinners into paradise regained. He did this by being lifted up on His cross.

AFFIRMATION
When I survey the wondrous cross, I see
Jesus dying to lift me to eternal life.

MORE WORDS OF HOPE
"The Spirit of the Lord is upon me, because he has
anointed me to preach good news to the poor. He has
sent me to proclaim release to the captives and recovering
of sight to the blind, to set at liberty those who are oppressed,
to proclaim the acceptable year of the Lord."
LUKE 4:18,19

THERE'S SOMETHING MISSING IN RELIGION

✝

HERE ARE FIVE PICTURES OF BARREN RELIGION: *Proselytism Without Conversion, Piety Without Charity, Authority Without Integrity, Display Without Devotion, Activity Without Humility.* We comment here on the last category of missing values—humility, true humility.

True humility is rooted in reverence for God and for persons. To be truly great is to be humble enough to be a servant. "The greatest one among you must be your servant." Matthew 23:11. An American college student visited the home of Beethoven in Bonn, Germany. Thinking that she was an accomplished pianist, she asked permission to play on the great musician's piano. After playing a few bars of *Moonlight Sonata,* she said to the guide, "I suppose all of the great pianists have played during their visits here." "No, Miss," he said, "Paderewski was here two years ago but said he was not worthy to touch it." To be humble means to be reverent in the presence of greatness. A humble person, then, has a sense of awe in the presence of Almighty God.

One deacon in an inner-city church objected to his church helping poor and hungry persons. He was shocked when his pastor told him who he really was. He said, "You are a deacon, meaning dia—through and konos—dust. It's the figure of a camel driver leading a camel through the dust while someone else rides on the beast of burden."

A young lady at confessional before her priest said, "I want to confess the sin of pride. When I look into the mirror I marvel at my beauty and cry out, 'How beautiful you are!'" The priest replied, "That's not a sin. That's a mistake!" But make no mistake about this—religion without conversion, charity, integrity, devotion and humility is so repugnant that it brings down God's judgment. (Read Matthew 23).

A legend tells of gifts being offered at heaven's gate in order to gain admittance. One came with a drop of patriot's blood but the gate did not open. Another came with a lover's lost sigh but the gate remained closed. A third came with a penitent's tear—the tear of an old man converted by a child's prayer. The gate swung open.

How shall we find what is missing? Jesus said in John 3:7, "You must be born anew." St. Paul wrote in II Corinthians 5:17, "When someone becomes a Christian he becomes a brand new person inside. He is not the same anymore. A new life has begun."

Something is missing. You can find it. Praise God!

AFFIRMATION
When I think of the wonders of creation,
it should not be difficult to be humble in
the presence of my divine Creator.

MORE WORDS OF HOPE
"Humble yourselves therefore under the mighty
hand of God, that in due time he may exalt you.
Cast all your anxieties on him, for he cares about you.
I PETER 5:6,7

THOUGHTS FROM
A GOLF COURSE

LAST MONDAY (FREE FROM THE OFFICE DAY), I FLIRTED with the idea of raking leaves (last year—110 jumbo bags!) Instead, I relaxed, installed a smoke alarm device, wrote letters, attended two meetings at the Augustana Home and made two visits there. Arriving home about 3:30 p.m. I found Marta raking leaves. I said, "Should I join you in raking leaves or will you join me in a game of golf?" We hurriedly left for the golf course with only one and one half hours before dark. We played under the pressure of this dead-line. Two balls went into the lake and two were lost in the leaves. And for the first time we lost the score card. Marta was winning so I was determined to find that card, thus avoiding any thoughts of voluntary versus accidental loss. After finishing the course, we went out looking for the card in the gathering darkness. I got lost. Coming back to the car we found the card under the windshield wipers. Evidently the friends following us on the course had found it. The card revealed that Marta had won by 7 strokes! Following the initial shock, I decided that I could not lose to a more attractive, exciting and "fun-to-be-with" partner.

I recall the story of a golfer who took a tremendous swing at the ball and missed it, as he often had done. Instead of hitting the ball, he hit an ant hill and many ants died. He took a second swing, missed the ball, hit the ant hill and more ants perished. There were similar third and fourth shots with the same results, until only two ants were still alive in the ant hill. One of the ants said to the other, "Brother, if you and I want to stay alive, we better get on the ball!"

Here indeed is material for a sermon. The title could be, "How to Stay Alive in a Dangerous, War-torn, Hope-destroying, Violent World." We find the answer in the Bible, 1 Corinthians 15:22: "For as in Adam all die, so also in Christ shall all be made alive."

How shall we stay alive in this world and in heaven forever? A familiar song will help us with the answer.

> He lives, and grants me daily breath;
> He lives, and I shall conquer death;
> He lives my mansion to prepare;
> He lives to bring me safely there.

AFFIRMATION
*Let's learn from tiny ants, golf games and,
above all, from eternal truth!*

MORE WORDS OF HOPE

"And you he made alive, when you were dead through the trespasses and sins in which you once walked, following the course of this world, following the prince of the power of the air, the spirit that is now at work in the sons of disobedience"

EPHESIANS 2:1,2

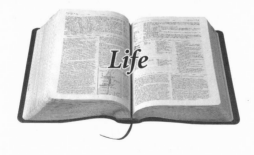

THOUGHTS ON THANKSGIVING

✝

LITTLE CHILDREN WITH THEIR VIVID IMAGINATIONS THINK of blessings for which to be grateful. A Sunday School teacher asked her class members what they were thankful for. One little boy said, "For my glasses". When asked the reason, he replied, "They keep the boys from hitting me and the girls from kissing me."

A father asked little Kathy if she didn't want to thank God for sending her such a fine new baby brother. Imagine his surprise when he heard Kathy praying, "Thank you, dear God, for Jimmy. And thank you that Jimmy wasn't twins like I heard the doctor say he might be."

A reserve officer, his wife and three children were living in a hotel near the military base. A guest noticed the soldier's little daughter "playing house" in the lobby of the hotel and said to her, "Isn't it too bad that you don't have a home?" The child replied, "Oh, we have a home. We just don't have a house to put it in."

These children found something to be grateful for. Do you recognize your blessings? Do you count them? Or are you too busy looking for things that are wrong? Will you join me in my "blessing list" and reflect upon them?

1. I'm grateful for the things I can get along without. We can get along without a lot of things if we find **All Things** in Christ. Let's be grateful, not for the abundance of our possessions, but for the fewness of our wants. Read Philippians 4:19.

2. I'm grateful that the irreparable past can be buried in God's love, and that He gives to me an irresistible future. Read about the blessing in II Corinthians 5:17.

3. I'm grateful that the promise of Romans 8:28 holds good

and that I have a God Who works **All Things** together for good as I surrender my life to His care and call and keeping.

4. I'm grateful that I have a Saviour from whom blessings continue to flow, not only for my benefit, but that I may share them with others. Please read Psalm 67. Why do we say, "Lord, bless me" in verse one? In order to share His way and His salvation with others!

AFFIRMATION
I'm grateful for all the things I can get along without in order to share gifts with persons in need.

MORE WORDS OF HOPE
"Blessed be the God and Father of our Lord Jesus Christ, who has blessed us in Christ with every spiritual blessing in the heavenly places."
EPHESIANS 1:3

TIME
FOR TURNING

✝

THE WORDS OF JOHN THE BAPTIST SHOULD BE FOR US A perpetual reminder, "Repent, for the kingdom of heaven is at hand." Matthew 3:2. God's Word makes very clear that we must face a time for turning or a time for burning. "Even now the axe is laid to the root of the trees; every tree therefore that does not bear good fruit is cut down and thrown into the fire." (Matthew 3:10). My friend, is there something you must turn away from in order to turn to God for healing and redemption?

I read some time ago of a business man who was running for a commuter train for his daily ride to New York City. People were still boarding as he came running. As he tossed away his cigarette he panicked at the thought, "That's my last cigarette. I'm clean out." He put his brief case down, rushed to the cigarette vending machine, fumbled for coins, put them in the slot, pounded the machine, swore, put in more coins, cursed and pounded until his hand was cut and bleeding, saw the train moving, ran, got aboard and sat down. Looking out of the window of the train, he saw his brief case on the station platform. This unhappy man lost his coins, his brief case and his temper. He had a bleeding hand and no cigarettes—a major crisis for him.

Someone may say, "Is Pastor Berg judging and condemning all cigarette smokers?" No indeed. It is neither my role or style to judge or condemn. I can share my concern about persons who subject their bodies to *unnecessary* cancer and heart failure risks in a day when these diseases have expanded into epidemic proportions.

My point in the illustration is that for every person there comes a time for turning in our Lord's plan of salvation. Some who are bound and defeated in their addictions may have to turn from cigarettes. Others may have to turn from rich foods and wrong diet and over-eating (big sins indeed!) Some may have to turn from pornography, from cheap and demeaning television programs, from addiction to material things and from gossip.

Someone may say, "How do you turn? We are bound and helpless." The answer lies in the word *Convert* which means "Con— with" and "Vertare—to turn." We turn **with God**. His presence and power make it possible for us to turn. Does your heart long for liberation and healing? Turn to God and His Word and watch Him work the miracle.

AFFIRMATION
I want to turn away from things that distress and destroy and look to Someone who can save and satisfy.

MORE WORDS OF HOPE
"If my people who are called by my name humble themselves, and pray and seek my face, and turn from their wicked ways, then I will hear from heaven, and will forgive their sin and heal their land."
II CHRONICLES 7:14

WELCOME TO GOD'S WAITING ROOM!

✝

LET'S REVIEW FOR A MOMENT HOW MUCH TIME WE SPEND in waiting. You wait for the bus—you wait for that telephone call—you wait for spring—for the elevator and for the clerk to wait on you. You wait for your check, for the traffic light to change and for the morning and daybreak. You wait for a friend, for the doctor and for payday. You wait for the baby to come. You wait for the mail and for quitting time. You wait for dinner time. You wait for company to leave. (Incidentally, some people bring joy wherever they go and others whenever they go.) It is possible that some worshippers wait for the sermon to end!

But isn't this what life is all about—to wait? In fact, today it is my privilege to welcome you to **God's Waiting Room**. The whole world is His waiting room, filled with people like you and me. Without this perspective of God's world, all of our waiting will end in devastating tension and frustration. We will wait for peace and miss the Prince of Peace. We will wait for freedom and miss the Liberator. We will wait for the ship and miss the Captain.

In 1972 Marta and I stood with 10,000 others in St. Peter's Cathedral in Rome. We were waiting for the coming of Pope Paul. The atmosphere was tense. Packed together and pushed, we waited. And waited. Then the trumpet sounded, the great velvet curtains parted, and the bearers of the papal throne came in spectacular array, with Pope Paul high and lifted up. People cheered wildly and flash bulbs made a panorama of light. In this setting I caught a vision of God's waiting room. I saw the King of Kings coming to His world with great power and glory. He came long ago as God's suffering servant and as Saviour. He comes each day in Word and Sacrament, in His Church and through His people. He comes at the time of our departure from this world. And He's coming again to reign forever and ever in the midst of a new heaven and earth.

A diary was found in the home of an aged woman who lived alone in poverty and illness, and who was found dead of malnutrition and possibly of loneliness. In the diary they read this identical entry on each of the last 30 pages, "No one came." I'm glad to be in God's waiting room. Each day's journal entry can read, "The King came today—He always comes."

Jesus says in John 14:18, "I will not abandon you or leave you as orphans in the storm. I will come to you." You never wait in vain. He always comes with everything you need. Everything! Praise God!

AFFIRMATION
Far more than waiting for the ship to come in,
I want to wait for the Captain of my salvation.

MORE WORDS OF HOPE
"But they who wait for the Lord shall renew their strength,
they shall mount up with wings like eagles,
they shall run and not be weary,
they shall walk and not faint."
ISAIAH 40:31

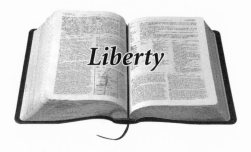

WHO BROKE
DOWN THE WALLS?

✝

A PASTOR VISITED A SUNDAY SCHOOL CLASS AND WAS invited by the teacher to question the pupils. "Who broke down the walls of Jericho?" the pastor asked. A little boy replied, "Not me—I didn't do it, pastor." The pastor, with a pained look, said to the teacher, "Is this kind of response typical in this class?" The teacher said, "Pastor, I know John is telling the truth. I'm sure he didn't do it."

The dazed pastor sought out the Sunday School superintendent and told him the story. He replied, "Pastor, that's our best class. I'm sure the teacher is right and that no pupil in that class is guilty." A few days later the burdened pastor reported the incident to the official Board. The treasurer quickly spoke up, "Pastor, I move that we pay for the damage and charge it to upkeep."

My friend, our Lord broke down the walls of Jericho to let His people into the Promised Land. Today, let us pray that He will break down the walls of the Church to let His people out into the world as His witnesses.

The true Church is the Church without walls—God's people serving with Him out in His world where our main work for Christ takes place. In the sanctuary with walls we are replenished and renewed, by Word and Sacrament, by prayer and worship, to go back into the world as Christ's presence and power. The Church with walls is there to prepare us for service in the Church without walls.

Worshippers leaving our sanctuary on Sunday morning see the sign that says, "The worship is over—the service begins." Someone has said, "The holiest moment in the worship service is when God's people leave the sanctuary to venture out into the world as His servants and witnesses." The Church which is the Body of Christ is God's lifeline to keep us going for Him in daily life in the world.

I recall a conversation with the owner of a pornographic theater located not far from our church. We wanted to buy his theater building for use in our community outreach ministry. I reminded him that this inner-city area needed a redemption center rather than the pollution center he was sponsoring. Then I added, "Here we stand side by side, two sinners who need a Saviour, both of us. I need divine help and you need divine help. He wants to use both of us for His glory and to help others. I believe that if you would surrender your life to Jesus and change your life, He would use you to change a big part of this city for God."

AFFIRMATION
God loves and welcomes everyone, but He loves
all of us sinners too much to leave us as we are.

MORE WORDS OF HOPE
"By faith the walls of Jericho fell down after
they had been encircled for seven days."
HEBREWS 11:30

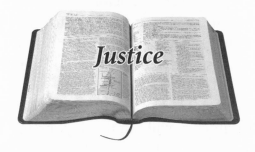

WHO'S AFRAID
OF THE LIGHT?

SOMEONE ONCE SAID, "A MOUNTAIN SHAMES A MOLE-HILL until both are humbled by the stars." Another said, "I have looked at the stars too long to be afraid of the dark." And another quote: "Don't criticize the person who is afraid of the dark. Try praying for the person who is afraid of the light!"

My friend, are you afraid of the light? The wise men of long ago were not afraid of the light. The Bethlehem Star brought them into danger. By their encounter with Jesus they risked death at the hands of King Herod. Are you ready for a personal meeting with the "dangerous Christ"?

The Epiphany light reveals your inner life. Are you willing to be exposed in your innermost being before a Holy God—to be serious enough about your infections of the spirit to seek health and healing? Or are you afraid of God's light? Do you prefer to curse the darkness? Will you respond to darkness or to light? Will you see the Great Light in the intense darkness, and follow it?

It is reassuring that the Light is more than a star or a candle. Which would a frightened child in the dark prefer—a flashlight or a loving hand? Would a crying baby prefer the principles of motherhood—or Mother in person? God's Light brings us to Jesus, the Light of the world! And there is no power on earth, no darkness, that can ever put out His light.

A merchant paid an enormous sum of money for a jewel case that was guaranteed to shine brilliantly in the dark. Eagerly he placed it on the table, turned off the lights and saw only blackness. But his wife read the instructions and the next night the jewel case glowed with dazzling beauty. The directions read, "Put me in the sun all day and I will shine for you all night." Will you stay in God's Word, my friend, in His presence, in prayer and worship and service? Will you walk in His light (I John 1:7), and let your light shine? (Matthew 5:16).

Jeanne had just been released from the Reformatory where she met Jesus Christ and was completely cleansed of great sin and guilt and made into a new person. Applying for employment she was asked for references. She had none. But she told one employer, "I do have one reference—Jesus, my Saviour. I know He will recommend me." The light of Christ in her radiant face got her the job! In the darkness keep looking at Jesus (II Corinthians. 4:6). Take His Word for it—His Light for it!

AFFIRMATION
I will find my way in this dark world
as I follow the Light of the world.

MORE WORDS OF HOPE
"The Lord is my light and my salvation; whom shall I fear?
The Lord is the stronghold of my life; of whom shall I be afraid?
When evildoers assail me, uttering slanders against me,
my adversaries and foes, they shall stumble and fall."
PSALM 27:1,2

69

WHY CLIMB
THE FENCE?

✝

MANY YEARS AGO, AFTER VISITING A MEMBER IN Deaconess Hospital, I was in a hurry to get to another hospital. I took a service elevator to the ground floor, went out the first exit I could find, and found myself in the inner courtyard surrounded by hospital buildings and the boiler and supply buildings. I encountered an iron fence and padlocked gate blocking my path. I walked to five locked doors at various locations, rang and pounded but no one came. I thought, "Surely someone will come by one of these doors and let me in." But no one came. I started to climb the fence but the barbed wire on the top made me change my mind. A preacher trying to scale the fence and caught in barbed wire at the top would not be a good Christian witness. Then I sat down on some steps to read. Finally I decided that I must get to Mt. Sinai Hospital. I went to the fence and was about to try to scale it when a door opened and a security officer came out. I said, "Sir, you really have a great security system here. I can't get out of this yard." He said, "Yes, you can. Just go through the gate over there. It opens from the inside." The gate that had appeared to me to be chained and padlocked could indeed be opened by the touch of the latch. I just had not tried it!

In Luke 7:11-15, we read about another gate:

> "As he [Jesus] drew near to the gate of the city, behold, a man who had died was being carried out, the only son of his mother, and she was a widow; and a large crowd from the city was with her. And when the Lord saw her, he had compassion on her and said to her, "Do not weep." And he came and touched the bier, and the bearers stood still. And he said, "Young man, I say to you, arise." And the dead man sat up, and began to speak. And he gave him to his mother."

70

Because people came through the gate, they met Jesus and a miracle.

There is no need to remain enclosed and boxed in by doubts and fears, lust and pride. The gate is open. Jesus is there to touch you with new life. Let us not try to gain freedom by climbing the fence of merit or self-effort. Go through the gate—the narrow gate of faith and self-surrender. You will be heading for a miracle—for sure!

AFFIRMATION
God's gate leads to a narrow way.
It is the way of the Cross that Jesus walked
and I want to walk this way with Him.

MORE WORDS OF HOPE
"Behold, I stand at the door and knock; if anyone
hears my voice and opens the door, I will come
in to him and eat with him, and he with me."
REVELATION 3:20

Church

YOU CANNOT CHOOSE
YOUR OWN RIVER

✝

AT FIRST NAAMAN WAS ENRAGED WHEN THE PROPHET
Elisha told him, a famous military leader in Syria, to dip down seven
times in the insignificant Jordan River (II Kings 5:1-14). He wanted
to choose his own river. He wanted to be healed on his own terms.
Could it be that many are sick in body and spirit because they cannot
see God's way of healing? Our Lord chooses the place and method of
healing. Just do what He says.

Many leave God's river too soon. Think of the tragedy of
Naaman dipping down six times and saying, "It's no use. I'm still the
same." We must go all the way seven times. There are no short-cuts.

Back in the early forties I was involved in a "short-cut" fiasco in
evangelism. In my former parish in Rock Island, Illinois, we decided to spread the Good News of the Gospel by dumping tracts, rolled
in bright cellophane paper, on 25,000 persons celebrating the city's
centennial in the downtown Market Square (we flew so low in the
tiny plane that we were reprimanded by the Air Patrol). How
thrilling it was to pour out the tracts. But the wind carried them all
into the Mississippi River. This dampened our enthusiasm. An
appropriate song to end the evening would have been, "Shall We
Gather At The River?" Shall we gather to be cleansed of sin and
guilt, of our human projections, of our love of ease and short-cuts?

In my Apartment Center, I have a 93-year-old friend who dis-
tibutes tracts. When he sees someone passing by him on a motor-
ized wheelchair he calls out, "Wait a minute. You are speeding. I
have to give you a ticket." Then he hands the person a tract. This
gives my friend the opportunity to witness for His Lord and
Saviour. This is a far better method and much more effective than
the one that is described in the story of the tracts landing in the
river.

The story of Naaman reminds us to listen to "little people" and to forgotten ones. A slave girl and Naaman's servants played a major part in his healing.

Finally, can you hear God's River of Life flowing by in our midst? **There is healing for you.** Turn away from your mirages and favorite rivers. Dip down in the old Jordan River. Plunge into the Fountain filled with blood and be cleansed. Then you will be ready at any time to cross the Jordan River into the Promised Land!

AFFIRMATION
When peace like a river attendeth my way,
When sorrows like sea billows roll;
Whatever my lot, Thou hast taught me to say,
It is well, it is well with my soul.

MORE WORDS OF HOPE
"There is a river whose streams make glad the city of God,
the holy habitation of the Most High.
God is in the midst of her, she shall not be moved;
God will help her right early."
PSALM 46:4,5

Blessing

WHY TAKE LESS
THAN THE BEST?

✝

IN ACTS 1:4,5 WE FIND THE GREATEST OFFER OF THE greatest gift, by the greatest of all givers. The apostles to whom the offer was made, apparently were willing to settle for less than the best. They said in Acts 1:6, "Lord, are you going to free Israel from Rome now, and restore us as an independent nation?"

They wanted a new nation. Jesus offered them a new spirit—a new life. He said, "You will receive power when the Holy Spirit has come upon you, and you shall be my witnesses" Acts 1:8.

The late Dr. E. Stanley Jones wrote, "Many a pastor asks for a change of parish when he should really ask for a change in heart. Many a congregation wants a new minister when it should really ask for a new Master. We are like the fever-tossed man seeking for a cool spot, first on one side of the bed and then on the other, forgetting that the fever is within him. We seek for a change of circumstances when our need is for a change of "inner-stances."

When the Holy Spirit came to the apostles they received something far better than a new nation and independence. They received a new community—the Church—and came under the divine control of the Lord of Glory who liberated them for the greatest conquest this world has ever known.

Another quote comes to mind: "Let us seek to abolish the slums of our cities. But what will this avail if we reject the gift of the Holy Spirit who abolishes the slum areas of the human heart? What good will it do to try to make a highway safe for travelers if Holy Spirit-less and unregenerate persons are thronging the Jericho roads of life?"

My friend, are you asking for less than the best? Are you asking for freedom from illness, worry, fear, insecurity, pain, people who upset you, or from whatever circumstances and environment you are in? You cannot be healed or helped or liberated until you ask for the best—the Holy Spirit. And that request will cost you your life. Our Lord indwells and fills only the life surrendered to His love and control.

AFFIRMATION
I want to desire the highest gifts.
The best gifts found in I Corinthians, Chapter 13.

MORE WORDS OF HOPE
"I have yet many things to say to you,
but you cannot bear them now. When the Spirit of truth comes,
he will guide you into all the truth; for he will not speak on his own
authority, but whatever he hears he will speak,
and he will declare to you the things that are to come.
He will glorify me, for he will take what is mine
and declare it to you."
JOHN 16:12-14

LOVE THAT LIFTS

✝

WE CAN LEARN MANY LESSONS FROM JESUS' WORDS TO HIS disciple, John, and to His mother, words spoken in the midst of terrifying agony as He was dying on the Cross. In John 19:27 we read the words of Jesus to His mother weeping at the foot of the cross, "Woman, behold your son." Then to John, the disciple, He said, "Behold, your mother." In other words, "Take good care of her."

Jesus died not only to forgive and reconcile and restore lost sinners, but also to set us free to take hold of ordinary tasks at hand—to help people in need—to give a cup of cold water—to bind up wounds—to feed the hungry—to find a home for a stricken mother. Jesus **ennobled** everything He touched. He ennobled the calling of a carpenter and the calling of a servant. He ennobled womanhood and motherhood—little children and family life.

Many years ago I was watching my wife, Marta, busily working on the typewriter. I said, "Do you know something? You ennoble the calling of typist. You also ennoble the calling of scrubbing floors." (She had also been cleaning the carpet that night.) It's true. She ennobled washing dishes, cooking and shopping. A burlap sack dress that she wore while giving a presentation on Mexico—she even made that look great. She also ennobled a sack! I can say this not only out of my love for her (every year of marriage to her was more wonderful and exciting than the last), but because of God's love and Jesus' presence in her life.

Liberation movements have been used by our Lord to set countless persons free. But without spiritual perspectives, without a recognition of the divine image in every person and without the worth that Jesus' self-giving love places on the individual—any liberation movement can easily deteriorate and become progress in a downward direction.

As we surrender our lives to Jesus and to the control of His indwelling Spirit, He will give us His love and power, enabling us to help lift and rescue others as well as ourselves, and to help make things better for everyone. Standing beneath the cross of Christ and aware of how much He thought we are worth (worth dying for!) may we hear our Saviour say to us, "Take care of each other. Love one another even as I have loved you."

Affirmation
God's love lifts me higher but also lets
me live in the valley of human need.

More Words of Hope
"And the King will answer them,
'Truly, I say to you, as you did it to one of the
least of these my brethren, you did it to me.'"
Matthew 25:40

A CHARGE TO SEMINARY STUDENTS AND PASTORS

I charge you to preach the Word, the whole counsel of God, whatever the cost. For what shall it profit the Church if she perfects her techniques and has nothing to say? I charge you to remember the relationship between faith and works, as Martin Luther reminds us, "Believing in Christ as your Saviour means being a Christ to your neighbor."

I charge you to recognize your mission under God, not to make plans or programs or headlines—not to make friends, to make progress, but to make disciples of Christ. I charge you to call people to obedience to the ten commandments and to reject the new morality which affirms "the ten suggestions—take them or leave them."

I charge you to be as radical and revolutionary as our Saviour who so loved the world that He gave His life (John 3:16). I charge you to be as conservative and narrow as Jesus who said, "I am the way, the truth and the life. No one comes to the Father but by me." John 14:6.

I charge you to be willing to suffer anguish and hurts and pain with others as the late Karl Barth reminded us, "There will be no great music on the Church's lips unless there is a great anguish in the Church's soul." This means that you will share bread for the body and the Bread of Life with lost and dying persons across the world.

I charge you to proclaim the Gospel as simply as the little inner-city boy who looked at the Cross and said, "Take a look. Jesus is my Best friend!" and as profoundly as St. Paul when he speaks of sin and grace in his epistle to the Romans.

Does this charge reveal the kind of emphasis we want in our

Church? Is this the kind of ministry we are happy to invest in—our time, talents and money?

AFFIRMATION
*I have a charge to keep—to follow
and serve my God and Saviour.*

MORE WORDS OF HOPE
*"Fight the good fight of the faith; take hold of the eternal
life to which you were called when you made the good
confession in the presence of many witnesses.
In the presence of God who gives life to all things,
and of Christ Jesus who in his testimony before Pontius Pilate
made the good confession, I charge you to keep the
commandment unstained and free from reproach
until the appearing of our Lord Jesus Christ."*
I TIMOTHY 6:12-14

A SPELLING LESSON

✝

AN AGNOSTIC PROFESSOR LECTURED TO HIS STUDENTS ON the theme, "God is Dead!" Beneath the theme he wrote in large block letters on the blackboard, "GOD IS NOWHERE". His daughter, a Christian, came into the room and shouted happily, "Daddy, you've found God at last. That sign! It's wonderful! **GOD IS NOW HERE!**"

Many people know how to spell SIN and how to keep sin in their lives. If they could only know the Saviour who can take the big I, which is the center of sin, and turn it into an O, changing it into Son, God's Son!

And may we be sure to put the "Y" where it belongs each Christmastide. Many think only in terms of "ours", our gifts, our family, our friends. It's like the story of Linda who was distributing gifts to her family on Christmas Eve. While all were opening their gifts and shouting with joy, Linda just sat by her unopened gifts, looking intently at the Christmas tree with no gifts underneath and crying softly. When her parents asked why she was crying, Linda said, "I'm crying because it's Jesus' birthday and He did not receive a single gift." **O**ur or **Y**ours—mine or His?

Most people misspell Christmas. Did you know that it really is two words—Christ and mass, meaning celebrating in worship the presence of Christ?

Many years ago I gave to a seminary classmate, at the time of his marriage, a beautifully bound book bearing the title, *What Men Know About Women.* Excitedly he opened it, only to find every page blank! A rather absurd prank, but perhaps a reminder that the New Testament, without Jesus Christ, has only blank pages. You cannot spell Christmas without Christ. You cannot celebrate Christmas meaningfully without Christ in your heart as Saviour and Lord!

I hope that you will never spell Christmas like this: X-mas. What a tragedy to substitute X for Christ. You can at least make it a cross, which would mean the celebration of Jesus being born to die for our sins.

AFFIRMATION
*I'm grateful for the Bible where I receive help in
the understanding of key words in my faith.*

MORE WORDS OF HOPE
*Let us remember that the word "born" is spelled in two ways.
"For to you is born this day in the city of David
a Savior, who is Christ the Lord"*
LUKE 2:11

"Surely He has Borne our griefs and carried our sorrows."
ISAIAH 53:4

MY THREE-SIXTEEN WORDS OF HOPE

✝

"For God so loved the world that he gave his only Son,
that whoever believes in him should not perish but have eternal life."
JOHN 3:16

"By this we know love, that he laid down his life for us;
and we ought to lay down our lives for the brethren."
I JOHN 3:16

"Do you not know that you are God's temple
and that God's Spirit dwells in you?"
I CORINTHIANS 3:16

"That according to the riches of his glory he may grant you to be
strengthened with might through his Spirit in the inner man."
EPHESIANS 3:16

"Let the word of Christ dwell in you richly, as you teach and
admonish one another in all wisdom, and as you sing psalms and
hymns and spiritual songs with thankfulness in your hearts to God."
COLOSSIANS 3:16

"Now may the Lord of peace himself give you peace
at all times in all ways. The Lord be with you all."
II THESSALONIANS 3:16

"All scripture is inspired by God and profitable for teaching,
for reproof, for correction, and for training in righteousness."
II TIMOTHY 3:16

CREDITS AND ACKNOWLEDGMENTS

Eunice Mathews, daughter of E. Stanley Jones, has given permission to quote from her father's books.

I pay tribute to the unknown authors of stories and illustrations which could not be traced to the proper source. I apologize for any such instances. If you recognize an uncited story, please let me know and the publisher and I will be sure to acknowledge the author in future printings.

Other Books by William E. Berg

for more information visit **www.bergbooks.com**

Show Me the Way to Go Home
Journey to the Promised Land

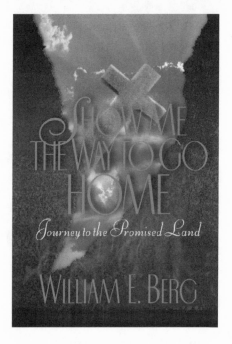

In this book, the author reminds us that the more heavenly-minded we are, the more practical our service will be in our Lord's work of healing and reconciliation in our broken world. He seeks to follow the Word of God Travel Service with Jesus Christ as Companion and Rescuer, and the Holy Sprit as Guide.

A Strange Thing Happened to Me on the Way to Retirement–
I Never Arrived!

At the age of 90, the author in this book seeks to redefine retirement. He insists that there is no retirement policy in the Kingdom of God. Difficult choices and impairments of body and spirit in older age are recognized. The divine dimension of life as revealed in the Word of God is highlighted.

Prayer in the Name of Jesus
and Other Writings

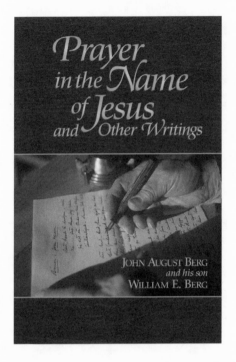

This book contains dramatic messages and stories from the lives of John A. Berg and his son, William E. Berg. John August Berg loved to walk. Walking and running with our Lord is the story of Amazing Grace and also the story of this book. Indeed, prayer is walking and talking with our Lord.

It's Okay Not to be Okay IF...

This is a book on the study of the *"Divine If's"*.
The author wrote this book not least as a safeguard
against the theology of cheap grace. Our God honors
us with the priceless gifts of accountability and
responsibility. He writes of the love of God which
provides incentive and power to respond to His
conditions.

Jesus
Final Authority on Marriage and Same-sex Unions

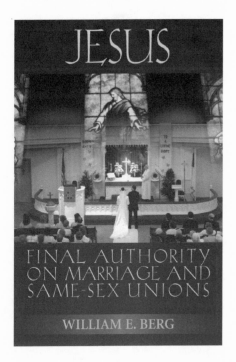

The title of this book may indicate to readers that its primary focus is on marriage and same-sex unions. Actually, the Word of God, reviewing Jesus as Final Authority, is the central message of the book. In the controversial issues of marriage and same-sex unions, we need to hear the Divine voice from heaven, "This is My beloved Son; listen to Him."

Trust Jesus
to Bring the Best Out of the Worst

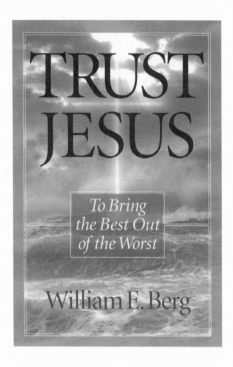

In this book, as we seek the guidance of God and His
Word, we hope to find answers to some of the dis-
turbing questions of our time: Where is God when
disasters take place? If Jesus is my friend, why doesn't
He take me out of my suffering? How does God
come into our lives and make His "best" possible for
us in every circumstance?